Simon Sterne, Thomas Hare

On representative Government and personal Representation

Simon Sterne, Thomas Hare

On representative Government and personal Representation

ISBN/EAN: 9783337152901

Printed in Europe, USA, Canada, Australia, Japan

Cover: Foto ©ninafisch / pixelio.de

More available books at **www.hansebooks.com**

ON

REPRESENTATIVE GOVERNMENT

AND

PERSONAL REPRESENTATION.

BASED IN PART UPON THOMAS HARE'S TREATISE, ENTITLED "THE ELECTION OF REPRESENTATIVES, PARLIAMENTARY AND MUNICIPAL."

BY

SIMON STERNE.

"Proportional representation is to our mind as evident and almost as important an improvement upon the majority system of representative government now in vogue, as the application of steam has been to industrial pursuits."—*Article by* PREVOST-PARADOL *in Journal des Debats, Feb. 18th,* 1870.

PHILADELPHIA:
J. B. LIPPINCOTT & CO.
1871.

Entered according to Act of Congress, in the year 1871, by
J. B. LIPPINCOTT & CO.,
In the Office of the Librarian of Congress at Washington.

TO

THOMAS HARE

THE FEW ORIGINAL IDEAS HEREIN CONTAINED

ARE DEDICATED

BY

HIS FRIEND AND ADMIRER,

SIMON STERNE.

NEW YORK, January 1st, 1871.

CONTENTS.

	PAGE
PREFACE	9
INTRODUCTION	13

CHAPTER I.
What is Representative Government? 19

CHAPTER II.
What should Representative Government be? . . . 46

CHAPTER III.
What are the Effects of the Present System of Representation? 64

CHAPTER IV.
By what Plan is a Proper System of Representation Attainable? 100

CHAPTER V.
Same Subject continued 135

CHAPTER VI
Other Suggestions for Reform 170

CHAPTER VII.
Application of the True Principles of Representation to Corporate Bodies 193

APPENDIX.
Hare's Electoral Law 213
Some Clauses of the Law of 1855 for the Election of the Representatives to the Rigsraad, framed by Mr. Andræ . 233

PREFACE.

The title-page of this work, before I determined upon the one which it now bears, gave me no little concern. As the first three and the concluding chapters are original, and the others rewritten, it would have been a manifest injustice to have printed the work as that of Mr. Hare; but then again I have used so much of Mr. Hare's book, and presented so many of his arguments, that to have left his name out of the title-page would have been, on my part, very like an attempt to obtain credit for what was in part the work of another. A history of the origin of this book itself will make clear the reason for the manner in which I have seen proper to present the arguments for totality or personal representation.

Some few years since, in conversation with Mr. Hare, he suggested to me the editing of his work on this side of the Atlantic, to which I consented, as my enthusiasm for his labors led me to believe that the work as it then stood would prove a success. Maturer reflection, however, convinced me that Mr. Hare's book, though admirably adapted to a philosophical student of Political Economy and the Science of Government, presupposes a degree of familiarity with English institutions and forms of administration, and a power to apply the reasons suggested by the evils inherent to them to our own modifications of these institutions, not to be hoped for from the average reader. Independent of this reason, there is another why the book in its English form would not answer our requirements. If we are a superficial, we are, at all events, a practical people, and the overconscientiousness of Hare's labors, the incorporation in his work of the clauses of a proposed electoral law embodying his reform, and the numerous and seemingly complex duties of the election officers (termed by him Registrars), gave to his exposition of the idea of totality representation an air of intricacy which has ever proved an almost insurmountable obstacle to the acceptance of ideas, which, in a simpler form and with less thoroughness in their presentation, would secure all but universal assent. Apprehensive that I might offend the susceptibilities of a friend and leader of thought, I abandoned the idea of republishing the book without stating to him my reasons for so doing. A few months ago it was my good fortune once more to meet Mr. Hare, and after a conversation having reference to personal Representation, I wrote the following letter to him:

"THE ATHENÆUM, Pall Mall, London,
April 13, 1870.

"DEAR MR. HARE:

"I feel that an essay based upon your work on Personal Representation, and giving a succinct account of all the modifications suggested by your continental and transatlantic disciples, would much aid the dissemination in America of a knowledge of the principles of Representative Reform.

"It would be necessary to leave out some of the chapters in your book and cut down some others, so as to make the whole of a size not too formidable for the courage of average readers. Of course I would not take such a liberty with the work of an author who is intellectually and personally so endeared to me as you are without his unreserved and fullest assent to his own dissection and dismemberment. Will you allow me to cut you down and up? and have you sufficient confidence in me to believe that I shall do it in the furtherance of science, and that your martyrdom will inure to the benefit of society? If so, say ay, and I shall mercilessly set to work.

"Ever yours,
"S. STERNE.

"THOS. HARE, ESQ."

To which I received, in reply, the following letter:

"GOSBURY HILL, Kingston-on-Thames,
"14 April, 1870.

"MY DEAR MR. STERNE:

"I am glad that you are about to bring forward a full exposition of the methods of personal, or rather, proportional representation. I commit my work, consequently, into your hands.

"When it was first published, now thirteen years ago, I was anxious to address every class of mind, and I therefore quoted largely from authors of various sympathies,—from Burke's Animadversion on the Defects of the National Assembly created in the Great Revolution, Guizot's Philosophical Disquisitions on Democracy, and Sismondi's Historical Reflections. I cited, also, much from Calhoun, who, looking at the rapid growth and power of the Northern States, had directed much attention to the preservation of what he regarded as the rights of the classes less numerous and powerful. All this had, I doubt not, an effect in some degree adverse to the reception of the principles I endeavored to propagate. My quotations were looked upon by many as appeals to this or that authority which they altogether repudiated, and they doubted, if they did not reject, a doctrine having, in their eyes, such questionable support. You will do well to get rid of such incumbrances, and I am therefore quite content that you should use your knife vigorously on the work of abridgment.

"Believe me,

"Yours, very faithfully,

"THOS. HARE.

"SIMON STERNE, ESQ., *Athenæum*."

Armed with this all-sufficient authorization, I determined to adapt Mr. Hare's book to American readers. As he, however, did not enter into the history of the institutions which he criticised, I began with the supplying of that defect, and was thus led on to present the subject from a somewhat different point of view than that occupied by him. A word of apology may be in place for dealing thus cavalierly with the work of an author which has received the highest commendation from authorities of the weightiest character, from John Stuart Mill downward. The justification of my course, however, will, in the main, after all said and done, depend upon the pages which follow these.

NEW YORK, Oct. 1st, 1870.

INTRODUCTION.

THAT there is all the world over a drifting toward the Representative System of Government, and a widening of the base of political power, by admission to political existence of a greater number of the subjects of government, is a fact patent to all observers of contemporaneous history. In England, recent reforms have extended the suffrage to thousands of voices which were heretofore never directly heeded in the business of legislation. In Germany, agitations, past and present, have admitted and do admit the people to greater and greater participation in political action and governmental power. In France, the empire itself based its right to existence upon all but universal manhood suffrage. And all other nations of the world laying claim to civilization are recognizing more and more the right of suffrage, and through it, the delegation of power to representatives. In our own country, we have, within the past few years, extended the suffrage, and by means thereof the basis of representation, to three-quarters of a million of people, who, theretofore, had not only not taken part in political action, but who had not even the free disposition of their labor, nor the free exchange of its results.

Representative Government, therefore, as the one important fact of contemporaneous political history, is so pre-eminent that every examination of its basis, its development, and its proper application, cannot but be of the utmost immediate practical importance.

That publicists and statesmen are fully alive to the importance of this fact is evidenced by the attention which the publication of Mr. Hare's book has awakened among them; by the numerous pamphlets, speeches, and debates which have grown out of the reform which he suggests; by the recent debate in Parliament upon the Minority Clause of the Reform Bill of 1868; by the debate in the House of Representatives upon the Distribution of Seats under the Census of 1870; and by the adoption of what is known as the Minority Clause in the new Constitution of the State of Illinois.

With the question of suffrage, as such, I have here no concern, whether it is a natural right or the investment of a political privilege, what should be its limitations, whether it should be extended to women and children, or whether it should be restricted, will form no part of this work. In its expositions of the evils from which we suffer reasons for or against any of these proposed measures may be found, but its primary object is the examination of the meaning of representation, the fact of representation as applied, the evils incident to the existing application, and the remedy.

INTRODUCTION.

The questions suggested by this examination are of such weight and import, of such comprehensiveness, that almost all the political questions of the day find a solution (at all events in part) therein, and the adoption of the remedy suggested thereby, would be, to use the language of an authority, "a specific against almost all the ills of government which are inherent to our own system."*

If any one doubts the importance of the subjects considered in the following pages, let him reflect for a moment upon the interests which in our own country are confided to representative bodies, and to the laws thence emanating, to which he is subject. In all matters pertaining to hygienic, criminal, and preventive police, he is dependent upon the representative body of his city or town; in all matters referring to his personal status, his property, and the laws which are to govern him therein, he is dependent upon the Legislature of his State; in all matters relating to his relations as citizen, commercially, as belligerent, or as ally, to the inhabitants of other countries, he is dependent upon the National Representative Chamber. Are there rights inherent to the citizen beyond those? Rights reserved to the people beyond and above representative control? In practice, none. Our bills of rights in our constitutions are so many requests, by the people to the legislative bodies, not to legislate upon certain subjects; but these requests have been generally disregarded when a strong tide of popular opinion has made it safe to break the restriction,

---

* Mill's Considerations of Representative Government.

as they lack the element which the Roman law calls *sanction,* i e. a punishment for the infraction, and an adequate machinery to carry such punishment into execution. Even if they possessed that sanction, it would always be in the power of another and higher representative body to alter, reject, and annul these restrictions whenever it suited the majority of the people to call such a body together. A constitutional convention, *also representative in its character*, deals absolutely with the powers of the whole people, and is, according to our practices, a sovereign, restricted only by the same power which holds the most despotic ruler in check—revolution. The powers which the judicial and administrative departments of the government wield are in fact subordinate to those of the legislative bodies. The recent conflict between the President and the legislative department of our country has proved this. The manner in which the judiciary were during the late war, and immediately thereafter, divested of some of their functions, clearly showed how delusive was the hope that that machinery, which was really or factitiously the direct exponent of popular will, could be withstood and held in check by the co-ordinate branches of government. It is foreign to the purpose of this work to enter upon the question, whether or not this tendency to the consolidation of power in the representative chambers is for the good of society. Its existence as a fact makes the inquiry of the proper formation of these bodies, and mode of election of their members, the one transcendent political question.

Since the publication of Mr. Hare's pamphlet, in 1857, and his book, in 1860, in which the subject of the election of representatives is treated in an exhaustive and masterly manner, so many plans have been suggested, and a few even tried, to arrive at a better formation of representative bodies, and a fuller and fairer exposition and mirror, than is possible under existing forms, of the popular mind, that the time is fully ripe for a treatise in which these various systems are set forth and their merits discussed. Chapters four and five embrace this part of my work.

It would be unjust to an American gentleman, Mr. J. Francis Fisher, of Philadelphia, not to admit that, even before the publication of Mr. Hare's pamphlet, in 1857, he had projected, and in a pamphlet, principally designed for private circulation, published a plan which was intended to secure a full representation of the whole people. Emile de Girardin, as early as 1850, in an article in the *Liberté*, seemed to appreciate the logical error of the present system of the partial representation of the voting population; but that most brilliant journalist and political writer had all the prescience of genius, but not the plodding patience of talent, to elaborate his ideas into a system for practical needs. Robert von Mohl, one of Germany's best publicists, has done much to lay before us the theoretical evils of a representative system based upon the counting, instead of the weighing, of votes; and Bluntschli, without directly advocating a remedy for the evils of existing representative systems, so suggestively arrays his facts that the reader feels the necessity for, and the practicability of, such a reform as Hare recommends. Of these plans and suggestions more hereafter, when I come to treat of them in appropriate chapters. I trust that sufficient has here been shown to prove that the questions before us constitute the very life of our political system : in the following pages I invite you to accompany me not into regions of thought which contain neither directly, nor scarcely remotely, anything of service for your practical needs; but I ask you to follow me into an examination wherein your own every-day experience can verify or disprove the correctness of my statements, your own sufferings, consequent upon the evils of our mistaken system of representation, bear witness whether a remedy is desirable, and your own knowledge of the advantages of right over wrong, truth over falsehood, can enable you to determine whether the remedy herein suggested be the true one. Mill says, "To inquire into the best form of government in the abstract is not a chimerical, but a highly practical employment of scientific intellect; and to introduce in any country the best institutions, which, in the existing state of that country, are capable of, in any tolerable degree, fulfilling the conditions, is one of the most rational objects to which practical effort can address itself."

CHAPTER I.

WHAT IS REPRESENTATIVE GOVERNMENT?

By government we mean that organism, whatever its form, which represents the absolute sovereign power of a people, and which enforces and receives from the individuals thereof habitual obedience.

This definition is true of all governments of which history gives us record. In the absence of all historical evidence of the organization of the first government, philosophers have invented a social compact to account for its existence. There is no basis for such an assumption; for when history began to transmit the traditions of peoples many governments, having a more or less complete organization, were already in being. The Books of Moses give us an account of the origin of the Jewish state, that was modeled upon the forms of the Egyptian government, which in its turn was probably copied from some older form, that of India; and the Vedas give us no account of the genesis of this form of government.

The historical school of constitutional and juridical writers regard, and justly, too, the question of the origin of government as an insoluble mystery, recognize government as an organism, having its justification for being by its universality, and the impossibility, under existing social relations, of masses of human monads thriving without an organism which embodies their totality and autonomy. The great divisions which embrace all forms of government are,—

I. Ideocracy (or theocracy), the government of a people by a god or gods through priests, who are the supposed direct exponents of his or their will. Whoever wield the governing power are invested, by the fancy of a barbarous and simple-minded people, with superhuman attributes, and as such hold absolute sway, until, by some oracular sentence, revelation, or other manifestation of divine will, they and their dynasty are deposed.

II. Monarchy, the government of a people by an absolute sovereign, who represents its totality, and who in his own person is the state: who reigns, but is not ruled.

III. Aristocracy, the government of a people by a class, or stock thereof, who, forming a minority of the whole, govern absolutely the remainder, though they are themselves, as individuals, subject to the rule of their class.

IV. Democracy, government by a whole people, either directly or indirectly through representatives of themselves. In democracy the relations of subject and ruler exist as much so as in other forms; each citizen, however, has the dual character of governor, as one of the collective mass, holding and wielding the sovereign power, and as subject in his individual capacity. As the whole people have never in any form of democracy taken part in the public management of their affairs, as we find in the purest of this form of government, subject races or classes, — a subjection depending upon social condition, color, sex, property, and intellectual incapacity, — it is difficult to distinguish, clearly and definitely, this form from an aristocracy. The difference is one represented more by the spirit which respectively sways the social organism than by the actual counting of governing and subject members. The aristocracy is based upon an assumption of an hereditary distinction between the higher and lower classes of human beings, and embodies and ossifies this distinction by rigid outward forms.

A democracy embodies the equality of the people, of each individual, and in its government claims to represent the community, as its forms may and constantly do expand to embrace such as were theretofore excluded from the governing power. All modern forms of government belong to one or the other, or are compounds of these various organic divisions.

It must be admitted that these divisions, sanctioned as they are by the authority of every writer on constitutional law from Aristotle downward, are subject to grave philosophical objections, but for the practical purposes of this work they are sufficiently correct, as the examination of the ideally best form of government is not part of our inquiry.

The constitution of the Greek republics, more especially the Athenian, gives us the democratic form in its fullest and most logical degree: the people (*i.e.* the freemen) legislated directly, and without the intermediation of any political machinery, to an extent theretofore and since unknown to political history. All important public questions were submitted to public meetings for discussion and decision; these meetings took place almost weekly. It is only by remembering that the Athenian slaves performed almost all the manual and skilled labor of the community that we can reconcile the fact of such general devotion to public life with individual prosperity. In these public gatherings of a people exercising the right of self-government, the ideal democracy found its first and only realization; at these the Athenian above twenty years of age felt himself a sovereign, and exercised personally all those duties which now devolve on the legislatures of republican forms of government. The characteristic traits of a democratic constitution, that the majority govern, were here fully developed; each citizen could speak, vote upon, or propose any law or resolution.

By the constitution of Solon, age had certain advantages in these gatherings, but in process of time these were swept away. The powers of these assemblies were, as is said of those of the British Parliament, omnipotent: Solon had, in the organic law, restricted them to the choosing of magistrates, the veto upon the administrative department, and the discussion of laws; but the Demos, feeling its strength, sweeping aside all restrictions, became an absolute despot, passing, by a majority, whatever laws it desired, and putting them into immediate execution. The actual framing of the laws was the duty of the

Homathetes, but their contents were dictated by the citizens in assembly, who not only legislated, but performed, in their collective capacity, many of the functions which we now associate with the administrative department of government. At these assemblies, the ministers of other nations delivered their messages and received their instructions; here peace was proclaimed or war declared; here Themistocles and Pericles received power to command; here the fate of conquered cities and provinces were determined and the spoils divided. The acceptance or rejection of new gods, the time and manner of the religious feasts, the rights of citizenship, and the penalty of ostracism, the levying of taxes, and the granting of subsidies; the manner in which the public funds should be expended, and the verification of the accounts; the building of temples, streets, walls, ships, etc.; all were here deliberated upon and determined,—ay, even the administration of the criminal law in important causes became part of the functions of this hydra-headed power. The Archons became (when the democratic element was fully developed) the mere servants of the people, and formed a powerless judiciary in the numerous courts wherein hundreds, and sometimes thousands, of jurymen determined the judgments and dictated the decrees of the judges. At Athens, the people (the citizens who were invested with the suffrage) governed; the whole people assembled, and a majority of the whole people concluded the measures which, as laws, were, in their individual capacities, to govern them.

The government of the people *by the people themselves* is possible, however, only when the territory of the republic is composed of one city, or is in so small a compass that the citizens can readily meet at stated and frequent intervals, and at times of unforeseen contingencies can be called together at the sound of a trumpet. A further condition of such a form of government is the necessary leisure on the part of the citizen to devote his thoughts and time to public questions,—a leisure possible only if the wants of the members of the community are but few and simple, and the laws to be enacted and enforced but few in number, or if the great bulk of the labor necessary to produce the commodities consumed by the people is performed by a subject race or class. For nations having an extensive territory, great variety and division of employment, and that intense competition in every human activity which make exclusive devotion to one business of life a condition of success, the form of democracy as the Athenians had it is utterly impracticable; such a people must, if they desire to preserve the democratic idea, do the work of legislation by deputies or representatives, and the business of administration by officers elected or appointed from time to time to administer this or that trust, and for the time being to wield this or that power.

Representative government, therefore, is not an original organic form, but a machinery necessitated by modern civilization and requirements of life to make democratic government possible,—a machine more or less perfect in proportion to its success in realizing the democratic idea of a government by the people for the people.

Wherever in modern times the democratic form of government has been adopted—with the single exception of the case of some of the mountain cantons of Switzerland—the sovereign legislative power of the community has been delegated to representatives; and the power left to the voter is generally only the selection of members of the representative body. So little did the ancients realize the fact of a representative system of government that even Aristotle said that a state should not be too large nor too small; it should not be so large but that all the citizens can be acquainted with each other, "for how else can they elect their magistrates?"

The representative system is the modern form of democracy,—and as such, a glance at the history of representation will enable us to account for the existence of our present method of election.

Montesquieu was right in finding the germ of modern representative systems in the forests of Germany; those sturdy Teutons who became the conquerors of Rome were the originators of the thought, "no taxation without representation." Their folkmote was not a city rabble, but a staid gathering of friends and neighbors, which not only satisfied the postulate of Aristotle, but went further, in never becoming even so numerous as to induce confusion. "To facilitate," says Mr. Chas. Goepp, in his admirable essay On the Legal Organization of the People, "the execution of his edicts, Charlemagne devised an expedient, which, possibly without any such design, constitutes the most important epoch in the history of the institutions under which laws are made. At stated intervals he sent messengers from his court into the counties, to confer with the counts and the people, enforce the render of services, collect such taxes as were then imposed,—most of them payable in kind,—promulgate the laws, hold courts, hear grievances, and either redress or report them to headquarters. This measure altered the county from a mere geographical division into a self-acting municipal institution. The messengers were received by the most influential inhabitants of the county, coming from every part of it, who thus constituted a natural representation of the people. The question of taxation kept alive the consciousness of a common interest as against the government. The coming of the envoys was the occasion for discussing, in this plenary assembly, all the affairs of the shire, for disposing of appeals from the hundred courts, and for addressing the king on subjects of universal interest. A connecting link between the hundreds and the king's court was established on the one hand, and on the other, the vast unwieldy ship of state was divided, like a modern steamer, into innumerable water-tight compartments, each of which could outlive the scuttling of any of the others and assist in floating them."

The empire of Charlemagne, as an empire, was short lived, because his successors lacked the ability required to perpetuate the throne. But the institutions on which that throne was reared, and which are really his handiwork, survived for centuries, and furnished the vital germ of those under which we are now living. The founders of England and Hungary regarded the great Frankish chieftain as the highest authority in matters of government, and organized the shires on the plan of Charlemagne.

On the continent, during the Middle Ages, the diets were meetings principally of the aristocratic classes, and not until the thirteenth century were the cities allowed to send a delegation of their leading burghers. The growing power, however, of the cities forced a recognition to representation, and though reluctantly granted, it was the entering wedge to the representation of the third estate. In England, the system of representation developed, as Hallam observes, partly from the fears entertained by the sovereign of the influence of a multitude who assumed the privilege of coming in arms to the appointed place. Long before the period referred to, we know that the earliest English kings not only acted on the advice and consent of certain persons eminently powerful among their subjects, but stated the concurrence of such persons in the official promulgations of the royal will, as giving it strength and validity, from their constitutional authority. Whatever were the qualifications of the advisers who surrounded the early Norman kings, they must have been expected to be numerous, since Westminister Hall was built by Rufus for their reception. The term Parliament was first used toward them in the reign of Henry III. "If there be any date in the early period of English History," says Mr. Cox, "which above all others deserves to be implanted in the memory of Englishmen, it is the year 1265,—the forty-ninth year of the reign of Henry III. Historians and antiquarians are agreed in referring to that epoch the earliest parliament of lords, knights, citizens, and burgesses. Before that time, indeed, there had been held many great councils of the nation, but none, so far as extant records show, in which the counties and boroughs of England were represented together."*

In the reigns of William the Conqueror and his immediate successors, councils were frequently convened, and were attended by the principal men of the kingdom,—bishops, abbots, earls and barons. The councils convened by the Conqueror, ordinarily at Easter, Whitsuntide, and Christmas, acted rather in an administrative than in a legislative capacity. The chief business of the councils of William I., so far as we have now records of them, related to matters of executive government, such as the grant of local charters and the decision of questions of title to land. The same observation applies to the reign of Rufus and several succeeding kings.

The first instance of a representative assembly is supposed to have been in 1213, the fifteenth year of King John. Writs were addressed to the sheriff of each county commanding him to cause four discreet knights of the county to attend the king at Oxford to consult with him on the affairs of the kingdom. No provision was made for the representation of boroughs.

---

* Antient Parliamentary Elections, by Homersham Cox. London, 1868.

This transaction took place two years before the Magna Charta, which was granted by the king at a great assembly of barons, held at Runnymede, in the seventeenth year of John (A.D. 1215). One of the provisions of this celebrated treaty provided that "no scutage which shall be imposed in the kingdom, except by common council of the kingdom, except to ransom the king's body, and to knight his eldest son, and to then marry his eldest daughter, and for this there shall be a reasonable aid." The articles in which this passage occurs constituted the original treaty between John and the barons of Runnymede, and are entitled "These are the articles which the barons require and the king concedes." The charter itself provides how this council is to be constituted "for holding the common council of the kingdom, for assessing an aid otherwise than in the three cases aforesaid, or for assessing a scutage, we will cause to be summoned the archbishops, bishops, abbots, earls, and greater barons by our letters under seal; and, moreover, we will cause to be summoned in general by our sheriffs and bailiffs, all those who hold of us in capite, at a certain day, to wit: at the expiration of forty days at least, and to a certain place; and in all letters of that summons we will express the cause of summons; and the summons being so made, the business shall proceed at the appointed day, according to the counsel of those who shall be present, although all the persons summoned do not attend." It will be seen that this council was to be convened for fiscal purposes only. The prelates, earls, and greater barons were to be summoned singly by royal writ, just as the members of the House of Lords are to this day.

The tenants in chief *only* are to receive a collective summons by the sheriffs and bailiffs. But in the next reign the principle of representation received a great development, much more nearly in accordance with the old traditions of popular government in the Saxon times. For example, in the year following the grant of Henry's charter (12 Henry II., A.D. 1226), a great council was held at Lincoln, which was attended by the representative knights of several counties, who accused the sheriff of infractions of the charters. The manner in which the knights were chosen shows that they are regarded as representatives. At a previous assembly of magnates at Winchester, the crown had agreed to call the Lincoln assembly; and for that purpose writs were directed to the sheriffs of certain counties, directing the election of four knights of each county by the milites and good men (*probi homines*) thereof. This assembly was called only for a special, though very important, purpose, namely, to examine complaints against the sheriffs of violating the charters. The Lincoln assembly was not a complete parliament, in the modern sense, but shows a great advance beyond the narrow system of representation contemplated by John's charter. It is remarkable that the electors included all persons comprised under the wide designation of *probi homines*.* In the thirty-eighth year of Henry III., A.D. 1254, the first repre-

---

* Cox's Antient Parliamentary Elections, p. 66, etc.

sentative council was assembled for the purpose of granting an aid. The sheriffs of each county were commanded "to cause to appear before the king's council, at Westminster, two legal and discreet knights, whom each county court was to elect for this purpose in the stead of the same." As yet there was no provision for the representation of boroughs.

Four years later, by the "Provisions of Oxford" (A.D. 1258), in a parliament, it was provided that in every county four discreet and legal knights should be chosen to inquire into grievances, and, upon oath, make a report on the same, which report, sealed with their own seal, and that of the county, was to be personally delivered by the sheriff to the parliament, to be holden at Westminster on the octaves of Michaelmas next ensuing.

We come now to the memorable occasion when the representation as well of boroughs as of counties appears to have been first instituted. In 1264 King Henry was taken prisoner. In the following year a parliament was held in London in obedience to writs of summons addressed in the king's name to a numerous body of barons, prelates, abbots, and other dignitaries, and also to the sheriffs of counties, and to various cities and boroughs. The sheriffs of each county throughout England were commanded to cause two knights of the more loyal and discreet knights of the several counties to attend at the time appointed. In the same manner summons were addressed to the citizens of York, the citizens of Lincoln, *and to the other boroughs of England,* to send on the aforesaid form "two of their more discreet and approved citizens and burgesses;" and similar writs were sent to the Cinque Ports, which are addressed to their barons and bailiffs, which command them to send four of their loyal and discreet men to treat with their prelates and magnates, and grant an aid.*

We thus arrive at the great epoch of the history of English representative institutions, of the summons of a complete representative assembly. The earlier parliament included only the barons and great men of the kingdom, except in the mentioned cases, when knights of the shire were summoned. Even the provisions of Oxford, which added greatly to the political power of the people, made no provision for the representation of towns. To ascertain the mode in which the election was conducted we must refer to the returns of the sheriffs of that period. They state the elections to have taken place in "full county court," or by the assent of the whole county. The right to vote seems to have been much more general at that early period of English history than it is now, notwithstanding the recent reform acts; and this right was restricted at a much later period than the period of the Third Henry (1216–1272), when all freemen were entitled to the suffrage, to wit: the statute of 8 Henry VI. (A.D. 1429), which limited the right of suffrage to those who are commonly called forty-shilling freeholders, and this limitation of the right of suffrage was the direct

---

* Cox's Antient Parliamentary Elections, pp. 68, 69.

cause of the decline of the influence of Parliament from that period down to the time of James I.

In 1295 (23 Edward I.) we come to another chief epoch in the history of parliamentary institutions, the regular and general representation of cities and boroughs. In that year the sheriffs received writs for the election of two knights of every county, and two citizens of each city, and two burgesses of each borough therein, with full and sufficient power for themselves and "communities" of their several counties, cities, and boroughs to do what should be ordained of the common council in the premises.

The reasons assigned by the king for convening this assembly are very remarkable. He recognizes explicitly the right of the whole community to be consulted on matters affecting their common interests. The commencement of the writs to the prelates runs thus: "Whereas, a most just law, established by the provident circumspection of sacred princes, exhorts and ordains that what affects all by all should be approved; so also it declares evidently that common dangers should be met by remedies provided in common." He then refers to a contemplated invasion by the King of France, with a very great fleet and multitude of armed men, with which he is about to attack the kingdom and its inhabitants, and if his power correspond to the detestable purpose of his conceived iniquity (which may God avert), to utterly efface the English language from the earth. The writ then proceeds to command the attendance of the prelates and clergy to treat, ordain, and determine with us and the rest of the prelates, chief men, and *other inhabitants of our realm*, how dangers and designs of this kind shall be obviated.

On the Continent similar efforts were made, by reason of the gradual development and progress of industrial pursuits and commerce, to organize a system of class and communal representations. One of the earliest, and at the same time one of the most important, organized systems of class representation we find in the Pyrenean peninsula. The kingdom of Aragon was in point of fact a republic with a king at its head. The nobility, clergy, and the cities were represented in the Cortes. The power of the Cortes was greater than that of the sovereign; the very words of homage with which the Cortes greeted its king is indicative of this fact: "We, who are on a level with yourself, who are more powerful than yourself, we raise you to the dignity of King, Sire, on the condition that you guard our rights; if not, NOT." A single member of the Cortes could, by preventing unanimity, practically veto a royal proposition. When any difficulty arose between the king and the Cortes it was referred to the Chief Justice (Justitia), who was independent of the royal power. In Castile, we find, as early as 1169, representatives of forty-seven towns in the Cortes. In 1315 ninety cities were represented. In the fifteenth century the Procuradores of the town had a majority over the clergy and nobility. The unfortunate jealousy of Burgos and Toledo, the feuds of families between each other, and against the citizens, led to the failure of the revolt of the cities against

Charles V., and the consequent downfall of their power.

The kings of France, during the years 1227, 1240, 1245, 1256, etc., called together the burghers of their "good towns" for the purpose of gaining their support by flattering their vanity. In 1302 Philip le Bel called together the third estates for the purpose of winning them over to his conflict with Boniface VIII.; and under Louis X., XIII., XIV., XV., and XVI. it was already an accepted principle that the estates had the power to vote taxes and subsidies. On the authority of Sismondi, Etudes, I., page 110, we have the fact, that in the republic of Florence in 1266 the whole population was divided into twelve corporations, called "Les Arts," with gradations dependent upon their relative importance from an intellectual point of view. The more important had special privileges accorded them, and they were permitted seriatim to nominate and appoint members of the administrative body. Each one of these guilds had its hall, where it elected its president and its representatives. Each was qualified to study its own interests, and to instruct its prior (who was a member of the board of magistrates) to further these interests and to redress its grievances. Each guild had its own military organization, its own flag, and the consciousness that it could resist, if need be, any infringement of its privileges. Thus science, culture, art, capital, commerce, and the lower industrial pursuits had a proportionate influence. All interests were consulted, and the final resolution depended more upon the quality than the quantity of the voters. Each Florentine, even the poor and ignorant, felt himself of some importance as a member of the guild; and still the sovereignty was not handed over to a majority, which in the greater part of our modern states are poor, ignorant, and incapable of forming proper political opinions.

In France, the Assembly of Notables, which was convened by Colonne on the 29th of January, 1787, was not a representative body. It was only after the first step of the revolution had been taken that the French Assembly became representative in its character. On the 21st of July, 1787, the province of Dauphin, without royal authority, convened its "ancient estates," and the nobility, clergy, and third estate met in friendly conclave. Brienne invited the provinces to meet, deliberate, and send deputies to the meeting of the estates-general of the realm, and Necker, in deciding that the third estate should send to the estates-general a number equal to the combined force of the other two estates, gave to the representatives of the people a governing power over those who in the convention sat in their own right. Even here the number of representatives was arbitrarily determined upon, their selection was left to the various modes of election known by tradition to the various provinces.

The Spanish Cortes is formed by dividing the country into provinces, each containing fifty thousand inhabitants, and each province being entitled to one representative. By the constitution of 1823, every Spaniard who had attained the age of twenty-five could vote at the election and become a member of the Cortes; the only qualification was this one of age. This system of universal suffrage was subsequently changed to a property qualification, which provided that no one was eligible to election or permitted to vote whose real estate did not yield a revenue of eight hundred reals.

At the time of the formation of our own constitution the several colonies had different qualifications of electors and a very varied system of elections.

The ideas of representative government and free institutions were developed to a very remarkable degree in the colony of New Netherland as early as 1645. By the eighth clause of the instructions of the commissioners of the Assembly of XIX., relative to the government of the colony, it was declared that "Further, inasmuch as the respective colonists have been allowed by the freedoms to delegate one or two persons to give information to the Director and Council at least once a year, of the state and condition of their colonies, the same is hereby confirmed."*

That the colonists were not contented with the simple right "to give information," but demanded a representative form of government, is indicated by the petition of the commonalty of New Netherland, etc. to Director Stuyvesant, in the year 1653, of which the fourth clause contains the following very remarkable words:

---

* Documents relating to the Colonial History of the State of New York, vol. i. p. 499.

"'Tis contrary to the first intentions and genuine principles of every well-regulated government that one or more men should arrogate to themselves the exclusive power to dispose, at will, of the life and property of any individual, and this by virtue, or under pretense of a law or order, he or they might enact, without the consent, knowledge, or election of the whole body, or its agents or representatives.

"Hence the enactment of new laws or orders affecting the commonalty or inhabitants, their lives or property, is contrary and opposed to the granted freedoms of the Dutch government, and odious to every free-born man, and principally so those whom God has placed in a free state or on newly-settled lands, which might require new laws or orders, not transcending, but resembling as near as possible, those of Netherland. We humbly submit that it is one of our privileges that our consent, or that of our representatives, is necessarily required in the enactment of such laws and orders."*

Another remonstrance of a like character, and of almost the same date, from the English towns of New Netherland, but written with more malice, shows that even at that early date the people attempted the formation of an assembly for legislative purposes. In setting forth the reason of their remonstrance, they say: "First, our apprehension of the establishment of an arbitrary government among us. Whether this apprehension be founded can appear from this: The entire government of this

---

* Documents relating to the Colonial History of the State of New York, vol. i. p. 550.

country is directed and controlled exclusively according to the pleasure and caprice of Dr. Stuyvesant or one or two of his favorite sycophants. Even if the Burgomasters and Schepens were sometimes summoned to the Council when occasion presented to dispatch business with the Director-General and Council, it is in fact rather to approve of his plans than to assist in consultation upon them; for, notwithstanding the Burgomasters and Schepens may dissent and differ from his opinion, the Director decides without them, declaring it must be so; and lastly, to show how great an appearance there is of the establishment of an arbitrary government among us,—it is considered sufficient that a Director, a fellow-subject of a free state, though filling a high and honorable office, with arrogant words disclaims his fellow subjects, who are assembled, with his previous knowledge, for the good of the country, and are thereunto convoked beforehand, by the lawful rulers of the first and most important city in this country, and present an humble remonstrance, declares their assembly illegal, protests against it, forbids the members and deputies thereof to meet again, orders and commands them to disperse forthwith, on pain of his highest displeasure and arbitrary punishment; as if they were by their acts guilty of resisting authority, and had conspired to revolutionize the state and reduce it under another ruler and government."*

When the colony came under English dominion

---

* New York Colonial Manuscripts, vol. i. p. 554.

they were for a short time deprived by the Duke of York of any voice in the making of their laws; but the merchants of New York, refusing to pay customs duties in 1684, were coaxed into compliance with the demands of the excise officers by the compromise of the re-establishment of the assembly. But down to the revolution of 1775 the right accorded to the counties to two representatives was not granted them as a matter of right, but entirely as a matter of royal grace; for an instruction from the Privy Council to Governor Tryon, in 1765, while commending his action in the division of Albany County, goes on to say that the governor shall be careful not to allow the new county to send, as of course, the two representatives, but to summon them specially by royal writ, so that the colonists were not to forget that whatever freedom they had was subject to royal control.

The framers of the constitution of 1789 could not consider the question of representation from a general and philosophical point of view, but were compelled to accept the recognized modes adopted by the various States. When the first article of the present constitution was under debate, the matters which occupied the attention of the members of the convention was how to allay the jealousies of the small and larger States, whether there should be one or two houses, whether representation should, in one or both houses, be proportionate to the inhabitants, or the wealth, the extent of territory, or the importance of the various States,—these were the matters of vital moment. If we are surprised at the comparatively unphilosophical character of the discussion by the members of the convention, we must console ourselves with the reflection that they were practical men, who had to deal with communities who were welded, for a time, it is true, by a common struggle, but who were intensely jealous of each other, and the problem for them to solve was the formation of a constitution which would be acceptable, and not the construction of an ideally best form of government. "The plan," says Hamilton, "in all its parts was a plan of accommodation."*

Party government had not at that early period developed itself, and the extension it would take in this country, and the manner in which it would pervert and defeat the objects of the framers, were not foreseen. The useless interposition of an electoral college, in the election of the chief magistrate, would else not have constituted a part of that instrument.

After considerable debate it was concluded to have two houses: the senate to represent the States, irrespective of their size, wealth, or number of inhabitants, on which terms alone the smaller States consented to become part of the Union; and a lower house to represent the people of the United States. Our triple system of an Executive, Senate, and House of Representatives was not, as is commonly supposed, a slavish imitation of the English constitution, with its King, House of Lords, and Commons, but arose from the necessities of the situation, and as a compromise between the united colonies to

---

* Elliott's Debates, vol. ii. p. 273.

remedy the evils incident to the government as it existed under the articles of confederation. Mr. Madison, in advocating the popular election of one branch of the national legislature against the scheme of Mr. Pinckney, to have the members of the lower house elected by the legislatures of the States, says that "this mode, under proper regulations, had the additional advantage of securing better representatives, as well as of avoiding too great an agency of the State governments in the general one. He differed from the member of Connecticut (Mr. Sherman), in thinking the objects mentioned to be all the principal ones that required a national government,—those were certainly important and necessary objects, but he combined with them necessity of providing more effectually for the security of private rights and the steady dispensation of justice. Interferences with these had more than anything else produced the convention. Was it to be supposed," says he, "that republican liberty could long exist under the abuses of it practiced in some of the States?" The abuses to which Madison referred were the prevalence of faction, and the fact that in all cases where a majority are united by a common interest or passion the rights of the minority are endangered, and thus the different classes of rich and poor, debtors and creditors, the manufacturing and commercial interests, would be arrayed against each other in the various States; and the protection of the minority consisted in, as Madison supposed, "the enlarging of the sphere (by the formation of a House of Representatives), and thereby dividing the community into so great a number of interests and parties that, in the first place, a majority will not be likely at the same moment to have a common interest separate from that of the whole, or of the minority; and in the second place, that in case they should have such an interest, they may not be so apt to unite in the pursuit of it. It was incumbent on us, then, to try this remedy, and, with that view, to frame a republican system on such a scale, and in such a form, as will control all the evils which have been experienced."*

The plan, as finally agree upon, was, that the upper house should represent the States by two senators, elected by the legislatures of the respective States, and the lower house the people in the States in proportion to the inhabitants thereof—one representative to every totality of thirty thousand inhabitants, counting slaves at the ratio of five for three. The time, place, and manner for holding elections was left to be prescribed by the legislatures of the States, and no general law of Congress was made on the subject until June 25th, 1842; the rapid growth of the country in population made the ratio of one to every thirty thousand too numerous a House of Representatives, and by that law the ratio was fixed of one for every seventy thousand six hundred and eighty persons in each State. To this act was appended what is known as the districting clause, which provides that when a State is entitled to

---

* Elliott's Debates, vol. v. p. 151.

more than one representative, the number to which the State shall be entitled under the apportionment shall be elected by districts, composed of contiguous territory, equal in number to the number of representatives to be elected, each district electing no more than one representative. In 1850 Congress passed an act, by virtue of which the House was limited to two hundred and thirty-three members, and the number necessary to elect a representative was to be arrived at by dividing the whole number of people shown to live in the United States, by the decennial census, by the number of seats in the House, and the quotient to be the number of inhabitants which shall be contained in the congressional electoral districts. The States of the Union have followed, with remarkable unanimity (the only exception being the new constitution of the State of Illinois), in the formation of their legislative bodies, the plan of the United States Constitution, and have artificially districted themselves for representative purposes, giving to each district of a certain number of inhabitants but one member, and thus throwing the election of that one member necessarily in the hands of the majority of the district.

The right to representation, the right mediately to take part in legislation, is now not denied by the governing power of any Western nation of Europe, and is gradually becoming the mode of legislation in all organized and developed forms of government. Representative government is therefore, at the present day, a system which bears in all its parts the evidence of the but partially successful struggle of the people for self-government. In England, the universities (powerfully organized bodies), the towns, boroughs, and the shires are represented. On the Continent, whatever people or autonomies sufficiently powerful to be dangerous, and to make themselves felt in the state, are represented. Here, artificial local districts are represented, and not the whole people; the whole system is one which is at present without philosophical consistency or dependence.

CHAPTER II.

WHAT SHOULD REPRESENTATIVE GOVERNMENT BE?

In all nations emerging from the absolutism of monarchy to what is termed a constitutional monarchy, or monarchy mixed with republican institutions, the development of the representative system is a growth stunted by the uncongenial atmosphere in which it was placed. Whatever loudly enough or strongly enough demanded recognition received it,— some trading company, or other rich monoply having interests to guard and much property to be taxed, was sure of representation. The principle of a government by the people for the whole people is not recognized by these systems, and the criticism that they fall short of a proper representative organization, means but little. In a country like our own, however, based theoretically upon the equality of all in their legal and political status, the question of the ideally best system of representation becomes a pertinent and eminently useful inquiry, and the fitness of the machinery we have adopted to accomplish the ends of our system, a most important examination. There are two classes of objectors to all improvements to whom a passing answer may be of service: those who say, whatever is is right, and those who believe that the constitution of '89 is the embodiment of human wisdom, and that whosoever suggests an improvement is guilty of an act of impertinent presumption. With reference to forms and administrations of government, it would be far more correct to say, whatever is is wrong, than that whatever is is right. Government is the gauge of the barbarism of man; to the extent that he requires the collective force of the community as embodied in law to compel him to respect the rights of his neighbor, he is a barbarian, and not a civilized being. Armies, police, and the whole criminal jurisprudence are the straight-jackets of the people. As the principles of the utilitarian side of morality become better known to the average man, and he, by the aid of political economy and scientific ethics, becomes more enlightened as to his true interests, the domain of government recedes in the same manner as the domain of special providence has receded by the advance of knowledge in the exact sciences. Every system of government has its historic justification. It is a right in the same sense that every weed is a right; a right because it is the combined product of soil, atmosphere, and germ, and under given circumstances could not be otherwise: but cultivation will improve it, and also improve human institutions, as Mr. Mill pertinently says, "Everything which can be said by way of disparaging the efficacy of human will and purpose in matters of government might be said of it in every other of its applications. In all things there are very strict limits to human power. It can only act by wielding some one or more of the forces of nature. Forces, therefore, that can be applied to the desired use must exist, and will only act according to their own laws. In politics, as in mechanics, the power which is to keep the engine going is to be sought for outside the machinery; and if it is not forthcoming, or is insufficient to surmount the obstacles which may reasonably be expected, the contrivance will fail.

"When the instructed in general can be brought to recognize one social arrangement, or political or other institution, as good, and another as bad—one desirable, another as condemnable, very much has been done toward giving to the one, or withdrawing from the other, that preponderance of social force which enables it to subsist. And the maxim that the government of a country is what the social forces in existence compel it to be, is true only in the sense in which it favors, instead of discouraging, the attempt to exercise, among all forms of government practicable in the existing condition of society, a rational choice."*

As to the notion more or less prevalent among us that political wisdom acquired its maximum in the crania of a few score gentlemen, who met and deliberated upon the formation of a constitution for the then much disjointed and disunited colonies, it is difficult to know how to deal with seriously. Let us suppose each of those gentlemen to be as great a genius in politics as Watt and Fulton were in mechanics,—what would become of a manu-

---

* Considerations on Representative Government.

facturer at the present day who would use the steam-engine of the one, or the captain who would use the steamboat of the other, in competition with the last modern mechanical improvement? He would be in the bankruptcy court in a month; and yet it is this precisely which we do in politics. Those men did a useful and important work; but they were very far from creating an ideally perfect government, and if they had, it would have done little good, as the people then were not more fit than the people now for accepting such a work. That the framers of the constitution did not foresee the extent to which party government would be carried in the United States is clearly evidenced by the electoral college clause; it is just this party system which has corrupted, and threatens still further to corrupt, not only our government, but, through it, the people; and to remove that yoke is a more difficult task than the thirteen colonies had before them when they rebelled from the mother-country, and the attainment of success herein is a far greater step in the direction of human freedom than was gained by the successful issue of the War of Independence.

Nothing can correct the evils incident to our system of government so well and so radically as the logical carrying out of that system; we have failed, as all other nations have similarly failed, because we were false to those principles, unconsciously false, it is true, by reason of an hallucination from which it is the most difficult thing to awaken us; and he will not have lived in vain who can contribute to this awakening. We have confounded two independent and entirely different political ideas and processes—the right of representation and the right of decision. The principle of representation is based upon the assumed right on the part of the citizen to take part in the business of making the laws which are to govern him; as there are practical difficulties in the way of his doing so, he must appear by deputy,—each man is entitled thus to appear by deputy. The machinery of representation, of voting, and of election is devised to accomplish this end. It does not accomplish it, it wastes from one-fourth to one-half the votes of a community: to the extent that it does so, it as effectually disfranchises the citizen as though a positive law disqualified him from going to the polls; it gives him the semblance, but deprives him of the substance, of his right. Even the majorities that are represented are unfairly and improperly represented, as the voter is compelled to sink his individuality, and oftentimes his best political opinions, for the purpose of belonging to the represented class. Why it does so, and how it does so, we shall presently see in the process of comparison between what representative government should be with what it is.

Mirabeau said, in a speech made in the Constituent Assembly on the 30th of January, 1789, and which is perhaps the most philosophical which that gifted orator delivered during his brilliant career, "that a representative body is to the nation what a chart is for the physical configuration of its soil: in all its parts, and as a whole, the representative body should at all times present a reduced picture of the people—their opinions, aspirations, and wishes, and that presentation should bear the relative proportion to the original precisely as a map brings before us mountains and dales, rivers and lakes, forests and plains, cities and towns. The finer should not be crushed out by the more massive substance, and the latter not be excluded; the value of each element is dependent upon its importance to the whole and for the whole. The proportions are organic, the scale is national."

The hallucination, or rather the hallucinations, which have prevented the representative chamber from being what Mirabeau says, and what we all feel that it should be, are, in the first place, that the right of the majority to govern carries with it the right of the majority to sole representation; and, secondly, that countries, States, districts, and counties have, as mere geographical subdivisions, interests distinct from those of the people who inhabit them.

To make clear the figment of majority representation, let us suppose that the city of Athens had grown to the dimensions of modern London, and the people had said: "We can no longer meet in the market-place, the time which should be taken up in deliberation is consumed by the counting of heads; besides, those who reside in the immediate neighborhood of the Pnyx are always at hand, while those residing at greater distances find it more difficult, and therefore are not so likely to attend, which gives to locality, irrespective of greater or less interest in the government, a meretricious advantage: let us devise some means by which we can participate in making the laws, and yet not have so numerous an assembly that deliberation becomes impossible." Let us suppose ourselves present at a meeting of the whole people, when the project of a representative body, to take the place of the popular assembly, is under discussion, and hear those astute Athenians discuss the question of the proper formation of the representative chamber.

Nikias rises and says:

"Brother Athenians:—For years past true deliberation upon laws has ceased. When upon some great occasion we all attend to assist in the making of our laws we form so numerous a body that not one-tenth of us can hear the speakers, and must vote therefore as ignorantly and prejudicedly, when the vote is taken, as though we had not been present; and a vote not intelligently given had better not be given. Besides, days are consumed in calling the roll of citizens and taking the ayes and nays; days which we can, all of us, expend better in our respective vocations; this is loss to those who attend, for which there is no corresponding gain. There is another loss to the Republic much greater than the mere frittering away of time,—the loss of our best men in these gatherings. The extension of our commerce with Samos and Corinth, the necessity for us to supply with wine and woven fabrics the people of Africa, have given to our best minds such active occupation that they are unwilling to lose the time now necessary for the transaction of public business; we see not the faces and hear not the voices of the best men of Athens: they are on the Areopagus, at the Agora, and at the Pireus, but we see them not on the Pnyx. In their places we have all the loiterers and idlers of the community, men of empty heads, who cannot succeed in the modern business of life, or whose parents accumulated by their industry enough to enable their descendants to live in idleness. Let us consider by what means this can be remedied; if we cannot remedy it, the Republic will die."

Diodotus rises. "The words of Nikias are words of wisdom: we all have felt these evils, but as they grew upon us insensibly they became of such frightful magnitude before they were observed that the danger of the downfall of the Republic is imminent. It is clear we can no longer come together to make our laws: not that the principle of our right to make our laws has changed, but that it is practically impossible for us to carry it out as we have done for three hundred years past. Our forefathers were few in number and had simple wants: they dressed in skins, and ate coarse bread and pounded meats. Each one of them could expend all the time necessary for public purposes. But modern civilization has changed this state of things. The invention of the handloom has altered the character of our wear, and the improvement of the wine culture and preparation has made us the exporters of wine to all other peoples. Employments have divided, and each freeman devotes himself to something requiring skill and foresight, leaving to the slave the rudest only of occupations; we would not, if we could, devote the time necessary to the public business, as individual prosperity is usually preferred to the general weal; and we could not, if we would, because our city has grown too large and its citizens too numerous to make a general attendance possible. But here let me raise one word of warning: our freedom consists in the right of each one of us to take part in these meetings. Let us scrutinize with care any plan which may be proposed, that it affect not this right, for if we part with it, our Republic is as effectually destroyed as though the usurper had placed his odious yoke upon our necks. We are not free if we are not permitted to make our laws; and each man is a slave who is excluded from that right; each freeman is the best guardian of his own interests, and if he is deprived of the power to protect these interests, they are likely to be disregarded and overlooked. Let us, then, proceed with care, else the liberty which we put into the machinery with which we intend to remedy these ills may be ground exceeding small, and much of it lost in the process. Let us see to it that we get out of the mill as much flour and bran as we put in corn."

Kleon, the leather-seller (the great demagogue, and the leader of the mob of Athens), now rises:

"Men of Athens:—I agree that we must adopt some other way than the present one by means of which the sense of the people is taken without their assembling here; this subject has occupied my mind for a long period,—in fact, ever since the last Olympiad, when we the people almost came to blows with the aristocratic and capitalist factions. I have therefore prepared a plan which will meet the difficulty, and shall proceed to read it to you:—

"The city shall be divided into two hundred voting districts of contiguous territory, so that all the interests of each district shall be represented; no district shall contain less than ten thousand voters; each district shall elect one member to a legislative body, upon which we confer all the rights we now possess; and that member shall be elected by a majority of the votes of these districts (see how jealously I guard the rights of the majority by this); these two hundred representatives shall be our legislators, and all the laws passed by a majority of these legislators shall be binding. We vote here by a majority passing the laws, we vote in the election districts by a majority in electing the representatives, thus the rights of the majority are protected; the representatives pass the laws by a majority, thus the rights of the majority are doubly protected. The minority cannot complain, as they are outvoted here in the popular assembly just as they would be in the district, and our law-making body is a manageable one. All the interests of the city are represented by the representation of all the districts of the city, and the majority govern. Each voter is represented, because he has the right to go to the polls and deposit his vote in the election of the representative; thus we have the problem solved, and that by the simplest possible machinery." Loud applause by the majority; cries by the Demos, "To a vote! to a vote!"

Thucydides here rises. "If the ancient custom of our Republic did not exempt words spoken here from judicial inquiry, Kleon should be brought before the Dikasteries as a conspirator against the liberties of his countrymen; no more ingenious device to despoil us of our rights has ever been brought before the public than this plan of Kleon. By an adroit confounding of the right to representation with the right to decision, which latter appertains to the majority here where each man represents himself, it is attempted, by giving exclusive representation to the majority only, to drown forever the voices of those who follow not the lead of Kleon. Let me remind you, citizens of Athens, why Kleon has, since the last Olympiad, cogitated upon this subject: you all remember the uneasiness which existed in the public mind, and the event which on that day almost threatened to array in hostile armies the freemen of our fair city. It was when, with undue haste and without that deliberation which the importance of the subject merited, it was determined by a bare majority, at the instance of this same man who now tries to cheat us of our liberties, to put to death the whole male population of Mitylene, and sell the women and children into slavery; and with unseemly haste was the swift trireme sped on its way to bear the direful message and our enduring disgrace in the eyes of all peoples. When the fathers of Athens went to their homes after this resolution, they felt that they had been cheated by their passions, which, artfully played upon by Kleon, led them into doing an atrocity unparalleled in the history of a civilized nation. We, the minority, discussed it, in the shade of the impluvium, with the majority when the passions were cooled, and on the next day it was manifest better counsel would prevail. It was then that the leaders of the majority of the day before determined that those who were in the minority should not have their views heard until the messengers of death were too far on their way to be recalled, and the deed of the murder of a people could not be undone. You remember, Athenians, how the lowest of the Demos stood in our way to prevent us from ascending to the Pnyx; but we were resolute. We resolved that this iniquity should not defile the fair fame of our history without a warning-cry from all who love our city, and we determined to die in defense of our right to be heard in opposition to a crime which would cease to give us the right to call upon our goddess for protection: we felt that the voice of reason must prevail even with the followers of Kleon. The majority attacked us at the temple of Theseus, but our compactness, the resolute bearing of our comparatively small number, made the issue of force doubtful; after a few broken heads, the Demos made way, and no longer opposed our right to be here, and our being here defeated this measure; and now, by an ingenious machinery of representation of a majority only, we are forever to yield to a trick of language, a cheat, and a snare that right for which we but two years ago were ready to fight, ay, and to die. Let me uncover this fraud and show to you that the day you make this representative scheme a law you will lose your liberties and open a Pandora-box of untold evils. In the first place, all those who are in the minority in the districts, are disfranchised, and those are the best among us; those whose voices we are always pleased to hear, and who speak words of wisdom unto us, will be silenced: we know how here the minority of the instructed carry with them a sufficient number of the majority of uninstructed to make good laws and defeat bad ones,—we did so in the third year of our war with the Peloponnesians; but this scheme will strangle those voices, by not admitting them to the law-making power, and allow them a simple choice between the demagogue of the masses or no representation.

"The voter who goes to the polls is not represented by the man against whom he votes, and who will probably suggest the very measures which the voter would have opposed here. Is the representation of the majority of the people a representation of the whole people? Even if we were to admit that for simplicity sake we will give to this majority a sole right to representation, and that the majority can safely dispense with that education on political subjects which, in every community, exists only in the minds of the minority, you do not at all, by the proposed scheme, secure the rule of the majority. This scheme proposes that after the majority have elected their representatives, a majority of these representatives shall make the laws; now add to the minority excluded from all representation, who may form almost one-half of the voters, that number of the majority who are represented by the dissenting members of the legislative body, and you place the law-making power into the hands of the representatives of the minority of the people. Therefore the proposed plan does not represent the whole community: it falsely represents the majority, and will simply transfer the whole political power into the hands of demagogues and their followers. (A voice. "The minority in one district may be the majority in another.")

"Do two wrongs make a right? Because the Demos, at the Stoa, will outvote the educated there, and thus disfranchise them,—in other words, deprive them of the privileges of freemen, is the mischief lessened if the same sort of oppression, as against the poor, takes place in parts of the city where the rich reside?

"Kleon artfully says that in cutting up the city into districts, all of the interests are sure of a hearing. This is a new idea in our politics; districts, so many acres of land, have no interests as such, the freemen therein have, and these freemen come here and represent these separate interests in their own persons when there are such interests; a circumstance which seldom occurs, as it is fortunately not often that a part of our city has an interest different from, and antagonistic to, the interests of the whole; and when such arise, no great harm is done if they are overridden, as they are generally dangerous; they are justly considered of importance in the scheme of Kleon, as that should be called a plan to foster and develop all the sinister interests of the worst elements of our body politic. Then, again, let me cast for a moment your horoscope: if Kleon prevails, you flatter yourselves that the best men in Athens will be the representatives. Never! the most popular men will, and such are very far from being the best. The men who are the physicians of our souls, who tell us unpleasant but wholesome truths, who stem and breast the waves of popular opinion when they run counter to their highest conceptions of right,—such men, the most useful among us in political life, will be doomed to silence and inaction. The oily-tongued flatterer, the wily corruptionist, the superficial gabbler, the panderer to the greed and lust of the majority,—such, and such only, will you have to pass our laws. Then there will be an evil which will arise from this scheme, the consequence of which it is easy to foresee: you divide the people permanently into majorities and minorities,—a division which is now but accidental, exists at the moment when we pass a law, is wiped out immediately thereafter; and the men who voted against each other on the project of sending our ships to Platæa, may vote with each other in the very next hour on a project for building a new temple for a victory to our arms, to our protecting goddess, Athênê. Give exclusive representation to majorities, and you create parties whose opposition to each other will be permanent; one opposing as a duty to itself all that the other party proposes, however beneficial that proposition may be for the public weal. You divide the people into two hostile camps, struggling with varying success for the mastery; and that struggle carried on, as it will be, with all the bitterness of party strife, with the use of every means, however unconscientious, will demoralize the whole community and destroy the Republic. Not only will the organized majority be a despotism compared with which the despotism of one man is as naught, for the despot must needs fear a people in revolt or the assassin's knife; but a majority is acted upon neither by fear nor by conscience. That minority who are now free voters, who openly speak their mind, will then become, when the majority is very great against them, and they are hopelessly excluded from representation, conspirators, who will sell themselves to different leaders of the majority. Parties, when about equally balanced, outbidding each other for mastery with corrupt bargains, or, when not evenly balanced, the one in majority an organized tyranny, overriding all constitutional checks; and the minority, a band of conspirators: such is the not very distant future which Kleon's plan is preparing for you. I too feel that with a constantly increasing population and territory we can no longer have the direct vote; and I also have a plan of representation, which differing, however, from Kleon's, will represent the whole community and be a miniature picture of the different opinions which for the time being exist in the minds of the people. My plan is, that the number of representatives in the lawmaking power shall be not more than two hundred, and as we have about two hundred thousand freemen in this city, that would give one representative to each totality of one thousand voters; thus each opinion among us, shared by the one two-hundredth of the whole people, is sure of a representative. There will not be majority and minority representation, but a representation of the whole people, and the law-making power will not, as in the plan of Kleon, be in the hands of a majority of a majority, but solely in the hands of a majority of the whole people. No votes will be wasted, and the franchise will, in every case, be a substantial right, and not a sham. Intellect will not be swamped by passion, nor capital by labor, but all interests find a representation in accordance with their relative importance in the state and their numerical strength. A carefully drawn law will, of course, have to provide for the duties of the officers of elections, and some provision should be made so that no votes be thrown away by the giving, on the part of voters, to any one representative more than the necessary number of votes to elect him. It will also be requisite to provide for the taking into the representative body of men not having the full quota of votes, after you have admitted those having the full quotas, so as to fill your representative house. Another plan, which will achieve the same result, and is less complex, is to regard each vote as a power of attorney, and allow none to enter the legislative body who holds less than one thousand of such powers, and then let the representative cast in the chamber either as many votes as have been cast for him or one for each totality of one thousand votes that he holds. The legislature would thus never have more than two hundred members, but might have many less than that number. But these are matters of detail, with reference to which we shall agree, if you are with me, that in changing our democracy into a representative government the whole people are entitled to representation, and that only where the whole people are so represented can the taking of the vote in the representative body be deemed equivalent to taking the sense of the people in general meeting assembled, as we are here now."

It is much to be regretted that the question of representative government was not presented to the mind of the Athenian public as I have imagined it to be, because their thinkers and enlightened statesmen would have given us doubtless as logically correct a model of a representative system as they have done of a pure democracy. Unhappily, representative government as it is, is the plan of Kleon, the demagogue. Representative government as it should be, is one which represents all interests and opinions of the community in proportion to their numerical strength, by some such plan as I have placed in the mouth of Thucydides.

CHAPTER III.

WHAT ARE THE EFFECTS OF THE PRESENT SYSTEM OF REPRESENTATION?

A PERFECT system of representation is plainly inconsistent with the exclusion of minorities; but the subject of representation would be very inadequately conceived if it were regarded as a mere question between majorities and minorities. The formation of electoral majorities and minorities is no more the natural means of arriving at political representation than it would be a natural result of any other association that it should be divided into two parties, one perpetually laboring to counteract the wishes of the other. The order and the occupations of mankind—the distribution of population and the supply of its necessities—are all provided for by physical and moral laws operating on the diversities of nature and of character which are found among men. These differences preserve the harmony and the vitality of social life. In political sentiment there is not less variety than in the other motives of human conduct; and abstractedly, it would be no more likely that the political opinions of the electors of a district should fall into two or three antagonistic divisions than that they should be composed of twenty, fifty, or a hundred distinct views or conceptions,—the dissimilarity would be much more probable than the similarity. Opinion and action in politics would be as various as opinion and action in other fields if there were not causes that enter into political bodies and create a disturbed and unhealthy movement, provoking antagonistic divisions. On the occasion of adverse desires in a society composed of many free agents, the majority must necessarily decide; but in the formation of a representative body, the purpose is, that the body thus to be created, and not the constituent body, is to be intrusted with the power of decision. If that were the function of the constituent body, there would be no necessity for appointing the representative. It is, consequently, by the majority of the representative body that the decision must be pronounced. It is the majority which speaks for the whole, and is irresistible. It may be likened to an engine of enormous power, which crushes all opposing forces. The election is the process by which this engine is constructed; but it is not essential to the efficiency of the engine that the same overpowering force should have been employed in the process of its construction. When the engine is formed, we require its power to be exercised; while the engine is being made, it is the engine we want, and not the power.

The conduct of men may be actuated by two different motives: one, the desire to do that which is believed to be right; the other, the desire to do that which shall be attended with direct success. At the time of an election, two questions may present themselves to every voter: the one, who is the person best fitted by character and talent to fill an office, in the duties of which the interests of the nation, to an incalculable extent, may be involved? and the other, who will my co-voters be most likely to choose? In other words, what is right, and what will succeed? It may be answered, that abstract right, when considered by a prudent man, resolves itself into a question of expediency and practicability,—that is, a case of compromise,—and that therefore the second question is that which such a man is justified in asking. It is true that in all political action you must consider what is expedient and practicable; this is the well-known defense of party action. Singly, one man can do little, and yet, by combining his efforts with those having similar objects, he may accomplish much. But it is necessary to consider under what conditions an individual is placed when he is called upon to yield up his own opinion of rectitude and prudence,—to what extent is the will at liberty? That which is a free concession among persons who have associated voluntarily to pursue the same objects and the same means, as the partners or shareholders in a company, or the members of a particular society, may be, and most commonly is, entirely different when the persons collected together are infinitely various in character, disposition, and object, and their association is compulsory, and not voluntary. In such a case the question ceases to be of the nature of a compromise, but becomes one of mastery.

Instead of yielding to the opinion of others, with

whom the voter has been led to associate, by the existence of some mutual basis of sympathy or harmony, he is, in the case supposed, obliged, in order to succeed, to give up his own opinions to those who form the most numerous portion of his co-voters, the greater number being, as one of the conditions of nature, the lower in capacity, and is obliged also to take into account all the disturbing and corrupting influences which may prevail. The necessity of obtaining a majority involves the necessity of creating a party, adopting a party name, and putting forward some party tenet or dogma: to all of which the majority must lend itself. It is not usually the political tenet which has caused the party, but the party which has created the tenet. In none of these things, any more than in the choice of their representative, can the members of the majority usefully ask themselves what they ought to do,—the only practical question is, what will be successful? Thus, the process of creating a majority demoralizes most of those who compose it: it demoralizes them in this sense, that it excludes the action of their higher moral attributes, and brings into operation the lower motives. They are compelled to disregard all individuality, and therefore all genuine earnestness of opinion; to discard their political knowledge; their deliberate judgment; their calm and conscientious reflection,—all must be withdrawn, or brought down to a conformity with those who possess the least of these qualities. The same injurious influences, in a measure, operate on the minorities wherever they make a decided stand for the purpose of contesting an election. The most intelligent will submit to the more numerous, except that in the minorities the greater apprehension of defeat may have led the more numerous classes within it to raise their standard of choice in order to increase their hopes of success. While this process of deterioration is going on among those who compose the active parties, a result even more fatal to the design of true representation is produced on another large, intelligent, and more scrupulous class of persons, who feel no disposition to make themselves the instruments of giving effect to the views of others with whom they have no common object or sympathy. These, therefore, take no part in the business of choosing those who are nominally to represent them. We find that in the densely populated districts nearly one-half of the voters are, for all useful purposes, in the same position as if they were disfranchised. A system which divides people into adverse parties—arrayed under formal names, which are themselves exaggerations, calculated to excite hostility where none really exists—has thus the effect of preventing the expression of the true and individual opinions of the members who compose either party. It lowers the force of thought and conscience, reduces the most valuable voting elements to inaction, and converts the better motives of those who act into an effort for success, and a mere calculation of the means to accomplish it. It is therefore not surprising that we hear of the infirmities of representative institutions, and that many persons should be able to look forward without terror to the aggravation of their more obvious evils, by any extension of some of the causes which produce them.

When we examine closely and in detail the evils incident to our own government by party, we shall see that they are mainly, if not exclusively, due to the partial and perfunctory system of representation we have adopted. Parties—extra-legal organizations of the people—are the result of the necessity for such organizations to acquire the right of representation. The law seemingly invests each citizen with this right; it actually does so, however, only on condition that he becomes one of the (for the time being) dominant majority in the district where he resides. To become one of the dominant majority, he must attach himself to the party in power, or to one which has the opportunity to come into power; to do so the voter must, in a majority of cases, surrender his individual preferences as to men, and as often to measures, which he believes to be for the public welfare, so that some of his opinions may prevail, or that some tenet of the opposite party, to which he is more especially adverse, may not become law. Let us illustrate the truth of this proposition by a few examples: A is a voter in the State of New York, in sympathy with the system of reconstruction of the Southern States adopted by the dominant majority in Congress; he is also a free-trader, and therefore opposed to the fiscal measures of this same dominant majority. The party place before him, as a candidate for the House, a Republican, who is a protectionist; if he deems free trade of less importance than the question of reconstruction, he votes for one who, as he well knows, will, in the representative body, vote for measures which A firmly believes to be pernicious and immoral. B is a voter in Ohio; he utterly detests the whole system of reconstruction Congress has seen fit to adopt, and believes the tenets of the opposite party, upon all the questions relating to the status of the citizens who had seceded from the government, to be the right ones; but this same party hints, in the campaign of his State, at repudiation, which may adversely affect his interests or revolt his moral nature; he casts therefore his vote for a representative whose whole course in Congress he deems dangerous and vicious, in order that that candidate shall not prevail who is pledged to a course which he regards as still more dangerous. The voter is not free; his vote, or rather the possibility of making it effectual, is fettered with a condition which makes the act of voting cease to be equivalent to an expression of opinion,—and the representative chamber thus formed, therefore, does not even meet the primary postulate of such a body —that it shall represent the opinions of the people whose votes elect the representatives. Even at the risk of being charged with tiresome iteration we are compelled once more to advert to the fact that, in addition to not representing the opinions of those whose votes elect the members of the representative chamber, the representative body does not represent, first, those who abstain from voting, and secondly, the minority, or possibly a majority, of voters who have voted for unsuccessful candidates. As it is generally supposed that the minority are represented because the minority in one district may be, and frequently are, the majority in some other voting district, we shall go into the question with figures drawn from our own recent elections to prove that this fallacy is not even approximately based upon facts, and that if it had such a basis, the present system of election is as wasteful of votes as it is utterly inadequate in causing a true expression of opinion.

In the election of 1868 the voters of the State of Maryland cast 92,798 votes, of which number 62,356 were cast for Democratic and 30,442 for Republican candidates of the legislative body of the State. Not a single Republican was elected, and the Legislature is composed exclusively of Democrats. The whole vote stood two-thirds Democratic and one-third Republican; the whole number of members of Senate and House of Representatives of Maryland on joint ballot is 111. A proper system of representation would have resulted in a return of 75 Democrats to 36 Republicans. By the return of members of one party solely one-third of the people of the State were, for opinion's sake, to all intents and purposes disfranchised. What a hue and cry would be raised against any one in that State who would propose that members of the Republican party should not be permitted to vote! And yet the law, under which this election was held and which made a different result impossible, gave to the deluded Republican voters the semblance and denied to them the substantial elements of the right of suffrage.

Let us now trace the consequences of this partial representation upon the probable legislation of the State. As a lie breeds lies, thus injustice breeds injustice. Let us suppose pending before this legislative body a law founded upon party spirit, and injurious in its ultimate effects to the whole of the people,—it is passed by a bare majority,—it becomes law because fifty-six Democrats voted aye, against fifty-five Democrats who voted nay,—can such a measure be deemed law made by a majority of the people of the State of Maryland? Had the 30,000 voters of the State who were disfranchised been properly represented, the result would inevitably have been the defeat of this mischievous law. The majority of a majority are, in almost every case, the minority of the people, and in the hands of this minority we place the law-making power by giving exclusive representation to the majority. It is an idiotic answer to say that the manifest injustice and undemocratic result of the Maryland election is equalized by a similar result in Maine, where, with a total vote of 94,182 in 1869, of which the Democrats polled 38,502 (considerably more than one-third of the whole vote), the number of members of the Legislature which they succeeded in electing were 37 as against 243 Republicans. Instead of this result a proper election would have returned 114 Democrats to 166 Republicans. Such two wrongs are very far from making a right. These consequences are by no means inevitable,—there are methods of making representation a reality, and every effort of the understanding should be brought to bear on the question of the adoption of the proper remedy.

Then, again, let us look at the percentage of votes cast as indicative of the interest taken in elections by the people themselves. New York State is taken as a fair type of the rest: In 1869 but seventy-one per cent. of the voting population voted; in 1862 less than seventy-eight per cent.; in 1861 but sixty-four per cent. of those entitled to the suffrage in the State cast their votes; and this voluntary abstinence from "exercising the highest duty of the citizen" arises mainly from the fact that many men, not liking the choice of evils which party machinery presents to their view, prefer to disfranchise themselves rather than become party to the elevation of unfit and improper men to political power. This loss of votes is of much greater consequence than would appear by a mere counting of percentage, as those who are guilty of this indifferentism are generally of the most calm and dispassionate as well as of the most instructed and thoughtful people of the Commonwealth. Countless exhortations of the party press, urging such men to take an interest in party politics and exercise their rights as suffragans, will ever prove unavailing so long as these very men instinctively feel that the exercise of this right, under its present form, is a delusion and a cheat. If they belong to the minority in opinion (a fact generally well known), they throw away their votes, as representation is denied to the minority. If they belong to the majority, they may be compelled to vote for men who turn uppermost in the machinery of party, and in whose professions that they will carry out the party principles they have no faith. In support of this I need but cite what Mr. J. Francis Fisher, one of our worthiest citizens, says in a pamphlet on Reform in Municipal Elections: "that, in the progress of years, when he wished to take his humble part as a constituent unit in the body politic, he found himself thrust aside from the procession of state as if he had no legitimate place in its ranks. At the various elections he seldom found any candidate presented to him whom he could sincerely approve; still more rarely one whom he could support with zeal. He always voted for those he thought the worthiest and generally without party prejudice, and the result was that he was almost always in the ranks of the defeated. Although classed among the educated and wealthy, he felt himself as much disfranchised as if he had been excluded from the polls by law. He had no voice in any nomination, only a selection among those he would not have chosen. Many of his most valued friends were in the same category, and with him almost despaired of redress."

A party composed of the most heterogeneous and antagonistic materials, bound together by circumstances having the force of law and told that they must act in concert and find one person who can reflect the most dissimilar things, can be compared to nothing better than the melancholy spectacle of subdued and torpid natures, which is sometimes exhibited by a showman in a cage as the "happy family," where every natural instinct is quelled and the weakest animal specimens of their respective species can solely be represented. With equal truth the other is called an independent voting district, where every man's action depends not upon himself, but in most cases on those to whom, of all others, he would be least willing to trust either his honor or his purse. To throw another ray of light upon one of the manifold forms of injustice, resulting from our present system, observe the exercise of power by the national Congress at the time and in the impeachment of President Johnson. When the framers of the Constitution gave to two-thirds of the members of the Houses of Congress the right to override a presidential veto, and to the Senate the right to remove the President by a like vote, after a two-thirds vote in favor of the impeachment of the supreme executive officer of the government has passed the House of Representatives, they clearly meant that, when the two-thirds of the people of the United States desire a certain will to be crystallized into law, the President shall not stand in their way; and that when two-thirds of the people, speaking through their representatives, shall believe that the President has been guilty of misdemeanors in his high office, and two-thirds of the States, speaking through the Senate, shall be convinced of his offending, he shall be removed. It certainly was not contemplated for a moment by the framers of our organic law that a majority of five per cent. of the whole popular vote should possess these extraordinary powers; and yet it is true that by means such as produce results in Maryland and Maine, heretofore alluded to, powers were exercised by the Republican party on the strength of a fraction not upward of a five per cent. majority, which were rightfully inherent only in a majority of thirty-three per cent. Should the combination of politicians known as Republicans feel pleased with this rich harvest of power which a five per cent. majority has yielded them, their pleasure may be lessened by the reflection that the combination of politicians known as Democrats will doubtless, under like circumstances, when they may be the "ins," use their power as fully and ingeniously against their opponents when they are the "outs." But the main and gravest charge against our present system of district, instead of personal representation, is the fact that it necessitates party, party organization, and their attendant train of evils. As party government is supposed to be an essential and beneficial concomitant of liberal institutions, let us see by what means, both in England and America, candidates are produced, what motives govern in their selection, and what we are to hope, and what we have had in the way of lawmaking from legislative bodies created by them. In examining English political life we must not lose sight of the places in which people meet, their habits and employments; and that the public-houses and beer-shops are places of great resort. This is due to many causes; much of it to the uninviting character of the vast number of dwellings in cities and towns not of the laborers alone, but even of the smaller tradesmen,—the mind yearns for some relief from sights and sounds ever sordid and discordant; much, also, is due to climate, which permits little social intercourse of any prolonged kind, except under the protection of warmed and covered buildings. An eminent English statesman, in one of his addresses on national subjects, lately remarked upon the difference between our modern life and public life in Greece and Rome, where the people conversed in the open air and under more favored skies. With us it is unquestionable that much of the time which the lower classes can spare from daily toil and necessary rest is spent in seeking ease and enjoyment in the houses which are thus provided for their use. It is there that they meet society of congenial life and tastes. Another feature of English life especially is its domestic character; this feature is predominant in the classes somewhat above the lower, and is more and more brought out as the depressing conditions of existence are removed. As a man advances in his pecuniary circumstances he gradually becomes less gregarious; his house assumes an air of comfort, furniture of mean appearance is exchanged for what is more elegant; his rooms are embellished with engravings or paintings that bring before his eyes some scene or tale touching some hidden chord and awakening thoughts deeper and higher than the counter, the workshop, or the desk has ever prompted; he loves his home as his home becomes lovely; his enjoyments, though intensified, are brought more within the narrow circle of his family and select friends. The refining process of society thus proceeds, and the coarser elements are left behind. They are left behind because their capacity for enjoyments has not been cultivated, and perhaps even the desire for them has, in many, been chilled and extinguished by adverse circumstances.

There are, also, many clubs and associations; of these are the numerous benefit clubs: the Odd Fellows, Foresters, and other societies, embodied under various names and rulers, and having many good purposes. In all these bodies there are some men who have gained an influence over others, to which they consciously or unconsciously more or less submit. The multitude thus form innumerable knots, linked and tied by the countless affinities and tastes which attract men to their fellows.

In every electoral district, in every community, some men will be found with penetration enough to discover the weaknesses, the follies, and the vices of their neighbors, and who are both skillful and unscrupulous enough to make them subservient to their own ends. These men are keen in the discovery of fit companions and tools for their purposes. "Noscitur a sociis" is a proverb. They form connecting links with another class of men which had grown up before the time of the English Reform Bill of 1832, and has since ripened and increased with great fecundity—a class of election agents. The election agent is in habitual communication with the cleverest and the most unscrupulous of those who are either themselves leaders or know how to tempt or cajole the most influential members of the various little knots or clubs which meet in the parlors and tap-rooms of every public-house in the district. The intercouse between the agents and the intermediate parties is kept up by many reciprocal services, by assistance in business, introduction to offices and employments under railway companies, in municipal and parish offices, and in other occupations in life, loans of small sums of money, and in infinite variety of favors of greater or less value. By this connection a machinery is ready at all times to cast a web over a very considerable number of the voters of the district, including, of course, a large number of the inhabitants who have no votes. It is time enough to make a distinction between the two classes when the net is to be drawn. We now come to the candidate. A general election is anticipated, and the aspirants for parliamentary distinction are brought into communication with the local agents. The candidate may be the director of a joint-stock bank, having a large credit given him by his brother directors; he may be an embarrassed man, seeking by a desperate effort to retrieve his affairs; he may be a roué, requiring a change in his method of dissipation; he may be a second or third-rate lawyer, hoping that the chances of parliamentary subserviency may open a road to promotion, which the legitimate labors of his profession are unlikely to afford; or he may be a wealthy man, moved by "a wish to garnish an acquired fortune with a little bit of ornamental dignity, or to lay the foundation of a successful career of tuft-hunting." Money, however, finds its way to the hands of the agents—money which has apparently nothing to do with the expenses of the election, and does not even come, by any direct or traceable means, from the candidate. It happens, however, that the parlors and tap-rooms become wonderfully animated. More refreshments are consumed, and nothing is said about the payment. These convivialities have ostensibly nothing to do with the election. There is no mention of any such thing; they are all in the way of good fellowship, and are matters into which nobody has any business to inquire. The time comes when the signal is to be given and the curtain drawn. The election is at hand; the approach of a first-rate liberal or a conservative of the purest water has been darkly announced. Perhaps an address, inviting the distinguished individual to offer himself for the representation of the electoral district, is got up, presented, and graciously responded to. But whatever be the course adopted, when the word is given by the chief agents to their inferior auxiliaries, a simultaneous concert bursts forth in praise of the candidate elect, and if the game has been played with anything like skill and liberality, he has already made such progress toward success as to render it very difficult for any adversary to displace him. The various steps have been taken silently and apparently without any plan or contrivance. Nobody knows how the candidate first comes to be thought of; nobody knows, of course, how the mantle happened to fall upon him; but the remarkable concurrence of opinion among so many persons, having no visible connection one with another, is to the simple-minded electors no small proof of his merits. It is easy to purchase the needful quantity of laudation and bluster. The hidden source of all this activity is known only to two or three, or, at most, a few of the initiated, who convert other men into their unconscious tools. "The corrupt lead the blind, and the blind lead one another." The candidate is instructed in what he should say, and more perfectly still in what he must not say. The proper insignia of party, whether liberal or conservative, the popular shibboleth, are settled and made the most of; and, unless the candidate be encountered by an adversary with more funds or better tactics, he embarks with every chance of success. In a general scramble for votes, with no trusted leader, it is not surprising that the most cunning and the most impudent should gather the greatest share. If, it may be asked, any of the electors, especially the more intelligent, be not satisfied with the candidates who have presented themselves, why do they not bring forward others? Why do they suffer themselves to be led or cajoled by a section or clique? To this question there are many answers: First, the machinery by which the candidates have been placed where they are has been carefully concealed. The foul play may be suspected, but it is not known and cannot be proved. Secondly, it is well known that when the ground is once occupied all attempts to introduce other candidates are nearly hopeless, and, if made, are sure to cover him who makes them with obloquy. He is branded as a traitor to the cause of his party; he is told that it will divide the interest and let in an opponent. It is clear, in fact, that every additional candidate, every step which would thus appear to afford a wider field for the choice of the electors, actually tends to defeat its own purpose, and more and more to extinguish the voices of the electoral body by throwing the election into the hands of the few, who, by the absence of all scruples, are held most compactly together. Thirdly, if he persisted in bringing forward another candidate, he would probably be met with the proposals of the fairest aspect; he would be invited to submit his candidate to a preliminary ballot, in which not only his more formidable adversary but some others should also be submitted for the choice of the party, and in which the phalanx of his chief opponents is, by previous arrangements, assured of an easy victory. Fourthly, if he still persisted in bringing another candidate to the poll, the language of invective would be exhausted to stigmatize the conduct of one who should thus, instead of submitting to party, think fit to act for himself. His personal quiet and repose would be destroyed, and the neighborhood, for a year or two at the least, would be too hot-to hold him. And fifthly, not only is the business of leading an opposition at an election one for which few men have at once time, talent, and disposition, but no man can bring forward an opposing candidate without subjecting him to considerable expense; and before a man will undertake such charges there must be more hope of ultimate success than the possession of senatorial qualities of ever so high an order would in such a case give. It is obvious that the practical difficulties in the way of the escape of individual electors by any efforts of their own from the power of an organized network of corruption are insuperable.

In our own country the system of party nomination and election was, until recent years, extremely varied. Before the war, in the Southern States, there was something like independent nominations; those who exercised the franchise were more independent of party domination than the inhabitants of the more densely populated Northern States, always excepting the tyranny of public opinion upon the subject of slavery in that section of our country anterior to and during the war of 1861–1865. In Massachusetts, until within a few years, at the town-meetings something like a nomination, independent of party managers, could take place; in some of the rural districts of Pennsylvania a vote is taken of the party instead of a nomination by delegates. But recent so-called reforms have almost everywhere, both immediately prior to and since the war of 1861, caused party management to supersede the popular freedom of choice; and the picture I purpose to draw of the system of party nominations is all but universally true.

The nomination for public offices is with us entirely in the hands of professional politicians. In our urban districts these politicians devote their whole time to the business of politics; in the rural districts the politician divides his time between the practice of the law, or the keeping of a grog-shop, and the manipulation of voters. The difference between the city and country politician is analogous to the difference between the city and country tradesman. For the same reason that the country tradesman cannot (on account of the limited demand) keep in his establishment but one class of merchandise, the illegitimate gains of office in rural districts are not sufficiently remunerative to justify exclusive devotion to politics as the business of men's lives. The difference between the two classes of politicians is not one of principle, but of opportunity. The men in direct contact with the voting element of the rural population are the loungers in the taverns of the small towns; there the half-educated lawyer waits for his clients and forms the acquaintance of those who are to aid him in his political ambitions. When he has a sufficient number of henchmen, upon whose fidelity he can count, he either secures a nomination for some small office in his county, or, what is more generally the case, places himself in correspondence with the general committee of one of the great political parties of his State; keeps that committee advised upon the political condition and election probabilities of his district, and is thus enrolled as a captain in that organization which, having its ramifications throughout the State, resembles an army of soldiers, with every conceivable grade and rank, from ensign to commander-in-chief. The holders of these posts are advanced only by giving proof of strict fidelity to party discipline, and by means of service in the party machinery or the controlling of votes and of money. It is by means of this machinery that, in the State of New York, a State containing almost a million of voters, the rival political parties can, by a careful canvass prior to a general election, calculate within a few thousand votes the number of ballots they can respectively cast. The general government of this machinery will either be in or gravitate toward the larger cities, for the reason that the more habile and astute politician is he who gives his whole time to this life, and that, as before observed, is only possible where the perquisites of office, as in cities, are sufficiently large to be a source of competence and of wealth. When a nomination is to be made of no special importance, the local politicians are permitted to have their own way; but for all higher public posts the slate is arranged at political headquarters, and the word of command is thence issued to place such or such a person in nomination; this command cannot well be, and is rarely, disobeyed. The local politician, being dependent for his preferment upon the good will of his superiors, is as little likely to rebel as the ensign of a military company against the orders of his captain. The political hierarchy imposes its yoke upon the leaders as well as the subaltern officers of the party machinery. It doubtless frequently occurs to these leaders that, as a matter of individual predilection, they would prefer to put some worthy and capable man, not a member of the organization, in a political position, but it cannot be done, because it would "demoralize" (make less faithful) their followers, for the self-same reason that a commander-in-chief would not dare to appoint a foreign officer, however great his merits, in command of an important division of the army. Every officer, from the general in the immediate way to the position thus filled by a stranger, down to the youngest lieutenant, each, would deem himself cheated out of his rights, and in the sense of feeling insecure whether he may not again have what he deems his rightful expectations disappointed, is therefore likely to lack zeal in the cause, and thus becomes demoralized. It is frequently a matter of surprise to foreigners, and unfortunately too often to our own citizens, that in our municipal elections we divide upon the same party lines as upon national issues. Why we should concern ourselves about the political opinions of the city chamberlain, treasurer, corporation counsel, or prosecuting attorney, any more than we do, whether he is a Unitarian or a Presbyterian in his religious convictions, seems a matter of just wonder,—the only proper question in such a case being whether the candidate is honest and capable. What a superficial view of the situation such surprise exhibits! The possession of these highly remunerated city offices and control of the vast funds in the city coffers are of vital importance to the political parties. By means of these, and these only, men can devote their lives to politics and perfect the machinery. The city of New York, for instance, raises by taxation and expends yearly about 20,000,000 of dollars. It is ordinarily supposed that about one-half of this is misapplied; however that may be, *the whole of that sum* is used to build up the organization. It is the life-blood of the party, and pulsates to the Rio Grande, precisely as the fat offices in large cities in the gift of the Federal power answer the same purposes for the same or the opposite party. It is for this reason that we cannot get rid of party in our local elections by the means we have heretofore seen fit to adopt. You cannot shake off the politician in the city, because the city's coffers give him control of the State, and it is just this rock which has shipwrecked all the efforts of well-meaning but short-sighted philanthropists in the direction of municipal reform. When the politician gives to you the city, he gives you the Malakoff of his position, and he will hold it just so long as our majority system of government makes party a necessity.

Having traced the building up of the party, let us see how the nominations are made, and how every element which should enter into the question of nominating men for public office is, by our system, carefully excluded. The leaders of the political parties meet in caucus, and determine upon the men who shall fill the various public offices,—this is called making a slate; when that is done, the trusty leaders of the various districts, precincts, and wards, if in a city; or townships, if in the country, are informed that they shall, at the meetings in their respective districts, send their delegates to a nominating convention of the party. These meetings, or primaries, are not recognized nor regulated by law. They are held at some obscure, and generally disreputable, tavern, so that the very meeting-place acts as a repellent against the influx of non-desirable, *i.e.* respectable, citizens. The form of an election is gone through with, and such delegates as have been predetermined upon are elected. Should, by any accident, a sufficient number of respectable people attend such a primary meeting, so that they could outnumber the hired ruffians of the party machine, the meeting is broken up by a fight, and the delegates are elected at some other meeting. Generally, however, it is not necessary to resort to this means, as the character of the place and the men who are at the bottom of the political ladder make these primaries sufficiently unattractive to those who love their lives, and have responsibilities which cause them not lightly to place themselves in jeopardy, to induce them to stay away. A convention thus made up proceeds to nominate officers; this same convention is packed, however, so that the whole nomination might be called a farce, if the perversion of the rights of the people to most sinister ends contained a single element of the ludicrous. The far greater number of members of the convention are either directly bought with money or promises of office. As a matter of accident, an honest man may be returned to a nominating convention; but as a general rule they are of the most pliant and corrupt of party tools. The men whose names are pressed for offices are either the party leaders themselves,—those who have control of the machinery of party, and upon whose will all the lower elements are dependent for promotion,—or persons who buy their nominations for money, or men whom it is desirable to enroll under the party banner, by reason of their real or supposed influence with some class, clique, religious sect or nationality, of which the people are composed, with the view to consolidate and perpetuate the rule of the party. With us there is very little direct bribing of the voter,—that species of corruption is more general in England than in the United States; but there is an almost invariable packing and bribing of nominating conventions, and, from an ethical point of view, it can make but very little difference whether the bribe is a direct one of money, or, as is usually the case, an indirect one of office, from the person to be nominated. The more customary manner in which men bring themselves to the notice of the political leaders is to show that they have a certain influence with a large body of men,—to that end they organize target and military companies, friendly and social societies named after them; their importance rises in proportion with the number of people they are supposed to control. Thus, in our dense centers, the representatives of distinctive nationalities, such as the German and Irish or religious sects, have a proportionately high value in the political scale.

After the party nominations are made, the leaders who have manipulated the selections set the same machinery in motion to "ratify" the nomination. The men who attended the primaries, and their friends, assemble in a great mass meeting, where speeches are made praising the candidates and reviling those of the other side; commonplace is talked about the principles of the party, rockets let off, much tar burned, and by means of this *deus ex machina* the people, or those who believe in the party tenets, are made to believe that the party nominations are somehow or other their nominations, and the candidates thus thrust upon them their candidates. They feel that men are selected for certain offices of whose fitness they have many misgivings; but to our busy people voting is enough of a task, and thinking upon subjects not directly connected with their business an almost intolerable effort. And thus this system of fraud continues and grows worse from year to year. To make independent, successful nominations is a hopeless task in opposition to the serried ranks of an army of hungry politicians fighting for bread. So many meretricious elements enter into the nominations for office that the question of the fitness of the candidate is hardly ever asked. The only question which may be considered of importance is the possible effect of his eminent and notorious unfitness. The political parties would not dare to make a city treasurer of him who had just served out his time in the State's prison for embezzlement or perjury, because they risk a defeat. They may also take a man who is peculiarly well fitted, because they wish to procure the support of the moral element of the community; this event arises, however, only when parties are evenly balanced. It may be objected that we have many men in office who possess the requisite qualifications for their posts—mere chance. Some capable men may be and are so ambitious that they are willing to walk the slimy paths of party to achieve political distinction; but, in doing so, they find it exceedingly difficult to preserve their sensibilities and refinement, or a keen sense of right and wrong.

The sketch we have made of party nomination is strictly true of the city of New York, and will become more and more true of other districts as they grow in population and divide employments, if a reform, radical in its character, but in strict accordance with democratic principles, does not emancipate the voter from party machinery and party control. Wherever the majority is not held in check by a minority of almost equal strength, it becomes a despotism, and a despotism not founded on the sentiments or traditions of a people can only perpetuate and consolidate its power by intrigue and fraud. Another evil incident to our present system, or rather the inevitable effect of electing the class of men which, as the French say, are possible under our party system, is the open and flagrant corruption of the representatives,—a corruption so universal that the very statement no longer excites repugnance. To charge a legislator with the selling of his vote seems as commonplace as to charge a harlot with want of chastity. Wealth, being excluded from its direct influence in electing representatives, uses the lobby as its indirect exponent, —the lobby is now all-powerful. To quote once more from the essay of Mr. Chas. Goepp: "Our railway companies, which originally were mere creatures of our legislative bodies, are now their masters. Moneyed men, associated under various titles, have gradually bought up, under the name of corporate privileges, the more important prerogatives of taxation and administration. A generation ago they approached the leading politicians as suppliants; now they hold them in pay, and use them not to extort further immunities, but generally to control the entire machinery of the body politic.

"These corporations are invaluable examples by which to study at once how power is attained and how it is forfeited. The influence of these bodies is found useless to those who are supposed to constitute them—the stockholders. As a general thing, the stock of every corporation is worthless, and under some qualifications it may safely be asserted that the more powerful the corporation the more worthless the stock. The stockholders have been served by their directors just as the citizens have been served by their representatives and politicians. The difference between them lies in this, that whereas the political representatives have seen their power and their profit slip into the hand of the directors, the directors have by no means surrendered anything to the politician. It is idle to speak of suppressing or even of discouraging or controlling corporations without first limiting the political power you delegate, and readjusting the distribution of political representation. They have become the sinews of trade, and trade is now the body of social life; ambition and administrative ability, jostled out of the management of State affairs, have come to feel that here is the real seat of power. He who controls a corporation has a share in the control of the world. Others make laws, but he dictates them; others influence elections and appointments, but he domineers over the elected and over the appointed; others reign, but he governs. A war on corporations at this day would be a war on the rulers of the country. The attraction of the green baize on the administrative ability of every republican country is so potent that the last two Presidents of the Swiss Confederation have successively retired from the head of affairs, in the one instance to govern a railway, and in the other to manage a bank. Now, what is the full import of these words? That we live in a republic? No; for the substance of power is not in the hands of elected officers. That our institutions are democratic? No; for the masses are not directors of corporations. That we enjoy equal rights? No; for the available rights are the franchises of the innumerable corporations, and these are as diverse as incongruous, and as arbitrary as accident, design, and corruption can make them. Our supposed republic is transforming itself into a congeries of little oligarchies, exercising powers as motley and as ill-assorted as the rights, privileges, dignities, and traditions of the German empire before its dissolution, with only this difference, that the manifold *imperia in imperio* are not territorial in their boundaries, but distribute themselves over the various branches of industry pursued by the people."

One of the most far-seeing and philosophical of America's statesmen, while criticising the decision arrived at during Washington's administration, through the personal and political influence of Madison and Hamilton, which gave to the President the power of removal of incumbents of Federal offices without cause and without consent of Congress, says: "Another of its effects has been to engender the most corrupting, loathsome, and dangerous disease that can infect a popular government,—I mean that known by the name of 'the spoils.' It is a disease easily contracted under all forms of government, hard to prevent, and most difficult to cure when once contracted; but of all the forms of government it is by far the most fatal in those of a popular character. The decision which left the President free to exercise this mighty power according to his will and pleasure, uncontrolled and unregulated by Congress, scattered broadcast the seeds of this dangerous disease throughout the whole system. It might be long before they would germinate, but that they would spring up in time, and, if not eradicated, that they would spread over the whole body politic a corrupting and loathsome distemper, was just as certain as anything in the future. To expect, with its growing influence and patronage, that the honors and emoluments of the government, if left to the free and unchecked will of the Executive, would not be brought in time to bear upon the presidential election, implies profound ignorance of that constitution of our nature which renders governments necessary to preserve society and constitutions to prevent the abuses of government."*

Every attempt at reforming this distemper referred to by Calhoun, under our present majority system of government, has proved a failure. No better example of this fact can be adduced than the history of the organization of citizens in the city of

---

* Calhoun's Essay on the Constitution and Government of the U. S., vol. i. Col. Wks., pp. 347, 348.

New York, called into being of late years, for the purpose of destroying the power and removing the spoils of the political ring of that city. The twenty-one well-meaning and rich gentlemen who organized that association had no higher purpose in view than to put better men in office. By an organized system of espionage and scrutiny of budgets and expenses, they discovered, or believed that they discovered, numerous frauds upon the city treasury. As the members of the executive committee of this association knew nothing of the business of politics, they were compelled to intrust the management of their campaign against corruption to men who, for an adequate consideration, were willing to make politics the business of their lives on the side of the responsible and wealthy tax-payers of the city. That organization soon in its turn became a political party, bargaining and huckstering votes for voices in the legislative and executive bodies of State and city. We have hereinbefore shown how the minority, when woefully in the minority, become conspirators; we find no fault with persons, but we have no words sufficiently strong to condemn a system of polity which demoralizes our very best men in the laudable effort to obtain their right to be represented. At a critical moment, when a division in the majority threatened to take the spoils from those who held them, the citizens' association, nay, its managers, had offered to them various offices in the gift of those who controlled affairs, and opposition ceased. Why should it not have ceased? Their object was to get better men in office; the citizen associationists were better men, and by acquiring office all that was intended was accomplished.

It is true that active opposition to the further nonfeasance and malfeasance of the politician is paralyzed; and when we approach him so closely, dine with him and vote with him in the same committee, this devil is not so black as he is painted. We cannot expect to do everything at once, and we are unctuously gratified that we have, at least, some better men in office. How differently would sound the words and be the tone of those very better men if they could have attained power, and held it, independent and without the assistance of the politician, by a plan of totality representation, which would have given to those whom that association represented a partial share of the collective governmental power of the community, greater than that for which they had to make bargains, which are in their very nature corrupt, and which tend to consolidate the power they opposed, by giving it a veneering of respectability it theretofore lacked!

That political knavery known as gerrymandering, which is possible only by means of, and is created by the district system, would, under totality representation, be utterly destroyed and laid to rest. Gerrymandering is the redistricting of States, so that the political majorities of contiguous districts not specially required for success therein, are made available by being added to the bordering districts to outweigh majorities theretofore given in such manipulated districts against the party having the power to gerrymander.

"In democratic government, the duration or uncertainty of the tenure by which its power is held, cannot of itself counteract the tendency, inherent in government, to oppression and abuse of power; on the contrary, the very uncertainty of the tenure, combined with the violent party warfare, which must ever precede a change of power under such governments, would rather tend to increase than diminish the tendency to oppression."*

This evil, so necessarily incident to the district system, would cease by means of personal or totality representation. Recent events, both in England and the United States, show how precarious is the tenure of office of the best and ablest among those who succeed in attaining it. Mr. Gladstone was twice defeated in the constituencies for which he had previously sat, and his exclusion from Parliament, though the recognized leader of its majority, was prevented only because the English elections are not simultaneous, and when his defeat became known, he could stand for some strongly liberal constituency where his success was assured by the withdrawal of the then running liberal candidate. Both custom and law have made such incidents irremediable when they take place with us, and the tenure of our legislator's office, however great his merit and his public services, is dependent upon the accident of the majority in his election district remaining of his way of political thinking. By means of totality representation the worthy legislator could never be

---

* Calhoun's Dissertation on Government, p. 24.

without sufficient support to elect him; and thus a political career would become an honorable vocation, in which the wisest and best among us could find a field of activity most beneficial to the community.

How different would be the political future of our country, if this reform were once fairly inaugurated! We would see the representative of every great living thought in our representative chamber. The masses would then, as now, send men who represent them; but instead of having the exclusive representation, their representatives would be brought in contact with, and educated by, the best intellects of the country in the representative body. And those who have had the inestimable advantages of being placed in daily contact with superior minds, know what a powerful educational influence for good, and restraining influence from evil, this is. Three honest and capable men in a body of fifty dishonest and ignorant representatives could check the designing and the knave.

By the proposed means, we provide an answer to the objections which may be urged with great force and truth to those extensions of the suffrage which have been proposed; that they threaten still farther to swamp the more intellectual and cultivated part of the community. Many an earnest, honest, and progressive thinker opposed negro suffrage by virtue of the law of self-defense. In a majority government, to extend the suffrage to the ignorant and the debased is not simply to take from the educated and the instructed the power of governing the ignorant, but it is to give to the lower intellect the government of the higher. The same objections hold true, so long as our present system prevails, to the extension of the suffrage to women. It would be an addition to the lower class vote. Substitute, however, personal representation for majority representation, and these objections fall to the ground. Intellect can send its own representatives, and these would wield in the legislative chamber an influence beyond all proportion to their numerical strength.

And lastly, what a magnificent gauge a representative chamber, in the event of the successful inauguration of such a reform, would prove of the actual state of public opinion and progressive education of the people! The system in vogue has given us corrupt party organizations and caucuses; causes primaries and party strifes, causes slates in conventions and political wire-pulling, and, what is perhaps worst of all, it causes sudden and almost violent changes of public policy by throwing governmental power from the hands of one unbridled majority into the hands of an equally unbridled majority, with principles of an exactly opposite character. The plans we shall offer emancipate the citizen from all these evils, and allow our governmental machinery to be improved in strict harmony with the moral and intellectual progress of the people.

CHAPTER IV.

BY WHAT PLAN IS A PROPER SYSTEM OF REPRESENTATION ATTAINABLE?

ADMITTING that each vote of the community should be made a substantial right by having assigned to it its proper weight and importance, and thus exercise a direct influence in the legislative chamber, and that the evils we have portrayed in our last chapter cry aloud for remedy, we have now arrived at the point of setting forth the method by which the one can be accomplished and the other cured. As we shall explain the various plans in all their details, this chapter will require more patient consideration on the part of the reader than the argumentative part of the work. It is only by its study, instead of casting over it a superficial glance, that the objection of complexity, which rises to the mind of every one when first confronted with a system of voting calculated to make the franchise a reality instead of a sham, will be thoroughly dispelled. I meet this one objection of complexity at the very threshold of this part of the inquiry, because it is the almost uniform objection to any substitution of the majority by the totality or personal system, and is one which suggested itself to Mr. Mill when Mr. Hare's plan was first brought to his notice. In an article in

Fraser's Magazine for April, 1859, since added to the second edition of his "Thoughts on Parliamentary Reform," he says "that he began with a great natural distrust of what seemed a very complicated set of arrangements, but he ended by being convinced that the scheme is workable, and is effectually guarded or guardable against fraud."

It is therefore not to be wondered at that minds having less grasp than that of Mr. Mill should require to put forth greater effort to master the details of the system, and thus at first blush urge the objection of complexity with greater energy.

This apparent or seeming complexity arises from the fact that everything appertaining to the exercise of the franchise is provided for by the law, and special clauses thereof take care of every vote. As compared with the system in vogue it is the complexity of a well-ordered farm, with its sheds and barns for different sorts of cereals, its stables and coops for different species of domestic animals, and its dwelling for farmer and laborers, against the simplicity of uncultivated prairie land.

The present system of election, though seemingly simple, is in reality more complex than that which is proposed to be substituted; for we must add to the law dividing the Union and the States into representative districts, and giving to each district but one representative electable by the majority, the very complex party machinery not provided for by the law necessary to obtain this majority. Even granting, for argument's sake, that the totality is more complex than the majority system, as justice, not simplicity, is the object of political institutions, we must adopt complexity rather than simplicity if the former achieves and the latter fails to accomplish that end. The Draconian code, punishing every crime with death, was much more simple than the modern criminal laws of the civilized peoples of the world, which assign to each crime a punishment proportionate to its heinousness; and yet how much more is true justice served by the complexity of these laws, as compared with the simple code of Dracon. To any one unfamiliar with the post-office system, how impossible it would seem to him that a few hundred clerks can, in a city such as New York, dispatch letters to upwards of half a million of post-office stations, and cause to be delivered to a million of people their messages from an equal number of stations during the period of a few hours. Would-be scientists frequently use the phrase that "simplicity is the law of nature;" the very opposite is true of all physical and social development. How complex is man, physiologically considered, when compared with the mere lump of protoplasm representing the lowest class of protists! How much more complex is the steam-engine than the stage-coach, and yet advancing civilization substituted the former for the latter! Differentiation is the law of progress, and if Mr. Hare's plan were as complex as its opponents declare it to be, it would not be an argument against its adoption so long as justice is better attained by its means than by the more simple process now in use.

The scheme of Mr. Hare is to substitute for the

dominance of local majorities a true representation of the people. It proposes that there shall be no compulsory union of the voters in particular districts, boroughs, or counties, although there shall be nothing to prevent them from acting together as at present, or to any extent they may desire, but that the measure of the constituency shall be the people and not the place, and that an equal number of voters, agreeing in the choice of a candidate wherever they dwell, shall be able to return a member to the House of Commons or Representative Chamber. It opens to every individual elector, whatever may be his condition in life, the means of exercising, in the nomination and choice of candidates, a discretion which is now possessed only by party leaders or persons having considerable local or public influence, or by what is with us called the caucus or managing committee. It adopts the principle that the voters of like qualifications are not better or wiser in one part of the kingdom of England or the United States than in another, but that wherever the voter may be he should have the same share of political power and the same inducement to give his attention and labor to public affairs.*

This permanent equality of political weight is obtained by dividing (by order of the Registrar-General appointed by the Crown, Governor, or President, and through the returning officers for each constit-

---

* Report on Mr. Hare's Scheme of Representation by Reform League, p. 5.

uency)* at each general election the number of electors who vote by the number of members to be elected, and permitting all bodies equal to the quotient who shall be unanimous in the choice of one candidate to form constituencies. Thus, if in England in the next general election for members of Parliament 1,316,000 votes are polled and the present number (658) of members are to be elected, 2000 voters will be enough to elect one member,—that number being the quotient of 1,316,000 divided by 658. If 1,974,000 should vote, the quotient will be 3000, who would then elect one member, and so on with any lesser or greater numbers. It will thus follow that every class of persons and all associations of opinion in number amounting to the quotient of 2000 or 3000, or whatever it may be, may be distinctly represented in Parliament by as many members as their classes or societies contain of such quotients. It need hardly be observed that the same process could be applied to the election of our representative bodies; it brings the disposition for voluntary association to the business of political life.†

If it is urged that such a system would delocalize the vote, the answer is that it would not delocalize, but free it from local slavery. As Mr. Mill, in his speech on the minority clause adopted in the D'Israeli Reform Bill of 1861, delivered in Parliament on the 29th day of May of that year, pertinently says: "It is objected that the plan destroys

---

* Clause 1, 2, and 3 of Electoral Law proposed by Mr. Hare, etc.
† Clause 4, 5, and 6 of same Electoral Law.

the local character of the representation. Every constituency, it is said, is a group having certain interests and feelings in common, and if you disperse these groups by allowing the electors to group themselves in other combinations, those interests and feelings will be deprived of their representation. Now I fully admit that the interests and feelings of localities ought to be represented, and I add that they always will be represented, because those interests and feelings exist in the minds of the electors; and, as the plan I propose has no effect but to give the freest and fullest play to the individual elector's own preferences, his local preferences are certain to exercise their proper amount of influence. I do not know what better guardian of a feeling can be wanted than the man who feels it, or how it is possible for a man to have a vote and not carry his interests and feelings, local as well as general, with him to the polling booth. Indeed, it may be set down as certain that the majority of voters in every locality will generally prefer to be presented by one of themselves, or one connected with the place by some special tie. It is chiefly those who know themselves to be locally in a minority, and unable to elect a local representative of their opinions, who would avail themselves of the liberty of voting on the new principle. As far as the majority were concerned, the only effect would be that their local leaders would have a greatly increased motive to find out and bring forward the best local candidate that could be had, because the electors, having the power of transferring their votes elsewhere, would demand a candidate whom they would feel it a credit to vote for. The average quality of the local representation would consequently be improved, but local interests and feelings would still be represented, as they cannot possibly fail to be, as long as every elector resides in a locality."

The seventh clause of Mr. Hare's Electoral Law provides that each candidate for the representation of any constituency shall send his name to the Registrar of London, Edinburgh, or Dublin, stating in his declaration for what constituency he offers himself a candidate, and shall pay to the Registrar the sum of £50. This fund, composed of the various sums contributed by the candidates, shall be used as the general election fund of the United Kingdom. The clause compelling candidates to deposit a sum of money toward defraying the general election expenses, has the effect of eliminating from the contest all those who have no reasonable probability of success.

Clauses 8 and 9 of the same Electoral Law provide the mode of publication by the Registrars in some certain designated newspapers of the names of the candidates who have offered themselves for election, and thus insure a correct list of such names in certain orders of preference. First, all persons who theretofore had seats in Parliament or Congress in the order of the respective length of the periods for which they have been members thereof, and as to new candidates, according to their age. Thus the duties of the Registrars in the promulgation of the names are so clearly defined that nothing is left to their discretion. Every step is governed by the rigid impartiality of anterior and positive law. Thus every elector, in addition to having, as at present, before him the addresses of the candidates of his own constituency, will be informed by an official gazette made public in every town and district who are the candidates for all other places. He will be able to make all the knowledge which he possesses of their character and reputation useful, as far as he thinks proper to do so, in the selection of the candidate by whom he desires to be represented. Sections 10, 11, and 12 of Mr. Hare's scheme, having reference to the abolishing of the liability of candidates for election expenses, and the abolishing of purely English disabilities, require no explanation in this work. Section 13 provides for the contingency of the election officer being himself a candidate by enabling him to provide a substitute. Clause 14 is of fundamental importance, as it defines the mode of voting. The vote will be given by a paper which may be called a voting paper or a balloting paper. The only essential peculiarity in the voting or balloting paper under this scheme is, that it gives the elector the means of adding to it the names of other candidates besides that of him whom he first and chiefly desires to select as his representative, so that not only every possible chance may be afforded of rendering his vote actually effective in securing the return of some one candidate, but also that he may be able to augment the moral weight of the statesmen in whom he has the highest trust, by placing their names on his voting paper, and thus adding to the amount of their popular support and to the parliamentary strength which they derive from this expression of the public confidence. The voting or balloting paper is proposed to be in the following form:

Name of voter.
Address.
Vote No.   , township of   , county of   .
　The above-named elector hereby records his vote for the candidate named first in the subjoined list, or, in the event provided for (statute), for the other candidates successively, in their numerical orders, viz.:
　1. Name of candidate.
　2. Name of another.
　3. Name of another.
　4. Name of another.
And so on, adding as many as the elector chooses.

The foregoing form, filled up with the names proposed by the voters, expresses in substance this: "I desire to be represented by the candidate whose name I have placed No. 1. If he should obtain his quota of votes before mine comes to be counted, or if he should fail to obtain a sufficient number, and therefore cannot be elected, I direct that my vote be transferred to the candidate I have placed as No. 2, and under the same conditions to candidate No. 3, and so on." Where the ballot is adopted, the words introduced for the identification of the elector, of course, will not be required. This list is entirely at the option of the elector to make use of or not; in his determination as to that he may be guided by his education, by his knowledge, by his opportunities, by the interest which he takes in public matters, in the well-being of his town, or in the welfare of his country. If he does not, or cannot, from the limited extent of his education or any other cause, make use of the information which is supplied to him by the gazetted lists as an aid in the performance of these great and solemn functions which his country has intrusted to him, he will still have in every respect, to the smallest particle, as much power in the exercise of his franchise as the existing system, or any other which has been proposed, can give him, having due regard to the equal and rightful power of other electors. He will have more of the just power of doing right, for the system here proposed would relieve him of far the greater part of the temptation which may be at present brought to bear on his hopes or fears, to induce him to swerve from what he may consider that he ought to do.

In striving to render the act of voting a solemn and deliberate act, we pursue an object which the greatest, the best, and the most scrutinizing minds, who have directed their thoughts to political subjects, have always regarded as of paramount importance. To whatever state of political society we look, whether to the present age or ages long departed, we find the same prevailing idea that political security and happiness depend on the degree in which the votes of a free community are regarded as serious and sacred things. Mr. Grote, in developing the history of the institutions of that people with which his labors have so indissolubly connected his name, describes it as a subject of just admiration that they "surrounded the delivery of the popular judgment with the best securities for rectitude, and the best preservatives against haste, passion, or private corruption."* Mr. Burke proclaims the foundation of the same great principle: "All persons possessing any portion of power ought to be strongly and awfully impressed with an idea that they act in trust to one great master, author, and founder of society. The principle ought to be more strongly impressed upon the minds of those who compose the collective sovereignty than upon those of single princes."† The power given to the voters, first, by the information which the gazetted lists afford to them of the persons who are candidates for the representation throughout the kingdom, and secondly, by the opportunity the voting papers afford of separating, distinguishing, and bringing out every form and shadow of political opinion, will give an immeasurable increase of force and strength to the true representative principle; and it will at the same time wholly extinguish the operation of the pseudo-principle of representation under which nations have suffered, and by which they are obstructed in their progress toward settled constitutional government. "In the present state of our

---

* History of Greece, vol. iv. p. 209.

† Reflections, etc., p. 138. See Mill, Considerations on Representative Government, ch. ii. iii.

knowledge," a late writer has observed, "politics, so far from being a science, is one of the most backward of all the arts;"* and certainly nothing can well be imagined more resembling a condition of barbarism than an election for a representative. Five, ten, or twenty thousand men, comprising every diversity of education, of thought, of moral quality, and of mental endowment, are called together to elect one or two persons to represent them. If they were only, as in old times, delegates to grant "a tenth or a fifteenth" for a foreign war, the representation might be sufficient; but a representation so created at this day, with all the varied questions which are opening and agitating mankind is a simple impossibility, and the name is a delusion. We are rejecting the aid of letters and the facilities of locomotion, ignoring the popular intelligence, and obstinately resolving to subject ourselves to the same difficulties as our ancestors struggled with when they had no roads to travel on, when not one in a hundred had learnt to read, and not one in a thousand had any book or manuscript to read if he had learnt. It is plain that as the intelligence of the country has advanced we have been receding from anything like a real representation, because it has become every year less possible for the rude forms of an earlier age to convey the varieties of expression that have in modern times been called into existence. It is no answer to say that if we have not had representation, we have had something that has

---

* Buckle's History of Civilization, vol. i. p 458.

done as well,—if it has not been actual it has been "virtual." The question is, whether we are to proceed toward a system of representation or a substitute for it. It is a question which every one should present to himself before he begins to reason on the subject of representative reform, as the whole tenor of his argument will be necessarily governed by the answer. It is also material to observe on this point that, while the present system induces a candidate, except in the case of a majority so compact as to be enabled wholly to despise and contemn the minority, to suppress and conceal some of his opinions lest he might lose votes by his candor, in the proposed method of election every candidate will be encouraged to express himself fully and distinctly, in order that he may be perfectly comprehended by minds in sympathy with his own; such candid explanations will have both an affirmative and a negative effect. Every elector will learn with more exactness who are those with whom he can more entirely agree, and with whom he totally disagrees. The encouragement afforded on all sides to truth will immensely increase the value of the evidence as to the real character and opinions of all who present themselves.

Section 14 of the proposed electoral law remedies this most important evil of the present system, that under the existing machinery of representation the amount of support which a candidate receives is entirely disregarded. No matter how great the majority of a candidate who is elected in any particular congressional district (a majority which may almost amount to unanimity), the vote of such member in the representative body is not one tittle stronger than that of him who has been elected by a majority of one. Clearly, therefore, every vote cast in excess of this majority of one is a vote thrown away. Mr. Hare's system provides a remedy for this waste of votes by counting for each candidate standing at the head of the respective voting papers simply the number necessary to make up his quota, and appropriating the remaining voting papers in which the name of such candidate appears at the head of the list to those who are the voters' second choice, etc. An example will best illustrate how this is done: First, we shall take the case of a large city—say New York. The city contains voters sufficient in number to elect ten members of Congress; and for these ten seats there are twenty candidates, whom we will name by the letters of the alphabet, A, B, etc. The professional, the mercantile, the manufacturing, and the working classes would all probably have among these candidates their favorites,—men who had addressed themselves to the questions in which the especial interests, or supposed interests, of each class are apparently concerned; and in framing their voting papers they would be likely to place the name of such favorite candidate as No. 1, still without withdrawing their support from other candidates with whom their general political opinions coincide. The names of such other candidates they might place in the order of their preference, as No. 2, 3, and 4, etc. Each voter might thus go through the list of candidates and place on his voting paper all the names of those of whom he approved. Voting places, each distinctly numbered, would be appointed in each district at which the votes of that district must be deposited, every paper being numbered consecutively as it is brought in. From these polling places the votes would be collected every hour and brought to the City Hall, where, under the superintendence of the mayor, registrar, or other election officer, the votes polled for every candidate (looking for this purpose only at the candidate No. 1 on each paper) will be arranged in a distinct heap or file in numerical order, as they were received at each polling place successively. Suppose these files, or heaps of voting papers, at the close of the poll to stand thus

A	30,000	L	1,500
B	22,000	M	1,400
C	11,500	N	1,300
D	11,000	O	1,200
E	10,000	P	1,190
F	5,000	Q	1,180
G	2,900	R	1,170
H	1,800	S	1,160
I	1,700	T	1,150
K	1,600	U	1,140

It will be seen that A, B, C, and D have many more votes than they will need, and therefore the candidates named second, or subsequently, on many of the papers, will probably have the benefit of the surplus votes. This will be ascertained as soon as the quota (explained before) is made known. Take it to be 10,000. In that case 20,000 of A's votes,

12,000 of B's, 15,000 of C's, and 1000 of D's will be liberated from the first three files, or heaps, and be applicable for the next person whom every elector has chosen to name.

Here the question again is commonly asked, which votes are to be set apart as the respective constituencies of A, B, C, and D, and which votes are to go on to the next candidates? It has been said that the files, or heaps, have been placed in the numerical order of the votes as received at each voting place, and then have been taken from each voting place in their regular turn. The mayor, or other election officer, will then take the 10,000 voting papers at the top of the file or heap of 30,000 given for A, which will be votes polled for him latest in the day, and these 10,000 will finally be set aside. In addition to this order of appropriation another rule is to be observed, which is this: that if any voting papers contain one name only, these papers must be taken for the candidate so named before any other paper with more names on it. Indeed, in such cases they can, of course, be given to no other than the single candidate named.

A stamp, " not required," will then be impressed across the name of A on the other 20,000 papers, and they will be used for the next candidate on each paper precisely as if the next name stood No. 1; and the same course will be pursued until all the papers above the quotas are redistributed as every voter has directed.

The result of the computation in New York City might stand thus:

A	10,000	O		2,750
B	10,000	P		2,500
C	10,000	Q		2,400
D	10,000	R		2,100
E	10,000	S		2,000
F	10,000	T		1,500
G	10,000	U		1,000
H	5,500	W		800
I	4,500	X		750
K	3,800	Y		700
L	3,690	Z		700
M	3,000	Z Z		600
N	2,750			

The mayor, or other election officer, of New York would then immediately return A, B, C, D, E, F, and G as duly elected, intimating that he has reserved his return of other candidates until the registrars or general election officers, meeting at some central spot, have ascertained and reported which of the other candidates have obtained sufficient votes in other places to make up the quota or comparative majority.

In order that this computation may be made, one or more of the election clerks, or other responsible officers appointed by the mayor or general election officer, will take charge of the voting papers polled for H and the candidates below him in the poll, and convey them to the central place indicated for the meeting of registrars, where they will be sorted and appropriated to the remaining first names on each paper.

The result of the ultimate distribution of votes may then be that the registrars or general election officers certify to the Mayor of New York that H,

I, K, and L have obtained the full quota or comparative majority of votes.

Sections 15 and 16 of the Electoral Law provide the time and place of the holding of the elections; sections 17, 18, 19, 20, and 21 embody the processes through which the voting papers pass after they have been placed in the hands of the polling clerks. These provisions have been explained by the example we have used. In the Appendix we give the draft law entire, as it may prove useful to legislators who may desire to legalize this or an analogous reform,—the proposed act drawn by Mr. Hare being a model of precision of language and of parliamentary style.

It may appear that it is entering into an unnecessary degree of detail to undertake the explanation of these minor arrangements of the business of the election; but, in truth, a closer consideration will show that there is no step which it is not important to make clear. Upon the establishment of a rational system of representation vast interests are depending. It is not possible to conceive any subject affecting the temporal welfare of mankind of greater importance, even if its influence wholly ended in time. The almost universal disposition is to turn aside from such considerations with the despairing cry that it is impossible to make the representation pure and faithful; and this despondence has carried away the minds of many persons in England to the ballot in the desperate hope that, by putting out that light which men have abused, virtue may be found in mist and darkness. We know how little the ballot has prevented corruption with us. In conveying to the mind, in the shape of a written narrative, the process of operation, every sort of machinery has an appearance of complexity. This would be immediately felt by any one who should endeavor in words to explain to another who had not seen it, the operation of Jacquard's loom or of the steam-engine. An attempt is, however, made to bring the proceedings of an election of representatives, such as it ought to be among an intelligent and free people in a civilized age, as vividly as possible before the eyes of every reader.

It is probable that the voting papers will sometimes contain the name of a person on the gazetted lists, who has not offered himself as a candidate for the particular constituency to which the duties of the returning officer exclusively refer, but whom, notwithstanding, the voter has, by selecting for the first place on his paper, proposed as a fit person to represent it. Where any such names occur first on the voting paper, the business of the returning officer will be to forward them to the general election officers. The returning officer is to confine his attention (except as to such transmission) to the voting papers in which the name of a candidate, or of the several candidates, for his particular constituency stand at the head; that is, are named successively one or two, or in any consecutive number, according to the voter's peculiar predilection, down to the point at which he introduces the name of one on the list who is not a candidate for his special constituency. As soon as such other name intervenes, a further combination is introduced, which brings the appropriation within the department of the general election officer.

It will be necessary to go a little more into detail as to the duties of those officers whom Mr. Hare calls Registrars, and who, whatever name we may choose to give them, are the general election officers of the State or country. As a large amount of clerical or mechanical labor will, of course, be necessary in dealing with the mass of documents thus brought to the offices of the registrars, an extensive building must necessarily be occupied as office-room for the few days during which the sorting and appropriating of the voting papers are in progress; but neither will probably be greater than is employed in the General Post-Office.

At the point to which the election is now supposed to have reached, the registrars, or election officers, have before them the certificates of the various returning officers and the voting papers which have accompanied them. Their duties, and the laws by which those duties are to be regulated, have now to be stated.

Some of the general officers' clerks being provided with tables of the names of the candidates arranged alphabetically at the head of distinct columns, the number of votes expressed on the returning officers' certificates to have been given for every candidate may be called over and speedily entered under the names of the respective candidates, thereby showing how many votes every candidate has received according to those certificates. This process, when completed, will show that many candidates who have been returned as elected by the constituencies which they named first in the gazetted list have received votes in other constituencies. This will doubtless be the case to a great extent with all men of high character and eminence. In all such cases the names of the members so previously returned will be canceled upon the voting papers in which their names are repeated.

The registrars, or election officers, have then to address themselves to the cases in which no returns of members have been made. The number of votes expressed in the certificates of the returning officers have now ceased to be guides as to many candidates, for, by displacing the names of the members who have been already returned, the names of other candidates are brought forward to the first place on many of the voting papers, which will make so many additions to the votes now to be counted for such other candidates. The extent of this alteration will be readily ascertained by the use of the tabular books of the election officers' clerks. Every clerk having the charge of the voting papers of a constituency will in a few minutes ascertain the numerical variation effected in those papers by the cancellation of the first names upon a certain portion of them, and can report the result of such alteration,—that is to say, what additions are thereby made to the votes given for other candidates. Additions will continue to be made in like manner as the other quotas are completed, and thus the name of every candidate having the quota will soon be ascertained. The completion of such quotas must then be certified by the election officers to the returning, polling, or election clerks of the several constituencies where votes for such candidates have been polled.

It is now necessary to prescribe other rules as to the order in which the votes shall be appropriated to the candidates where there are two or more constituencies involved, which candidates have, among the unappropriated voting papers, more than the quota of votes; and the simple point to be determined is, which of such votes shall be actually and finally appropriated to the several candidates having such excess of votes, and which of such votes shall go over to another candidate standing lower on the voting paper. The rules to be followed are laid down by Mr. Hare as follows in the 24th section of his proposed Electoral Law:

If the candidate be a candidate for the representation of several constituencies, and shall not have been elected as a member for the constituency that appears by the gazetted list to be the first constituency for which he has declared himself a candidate, there shall be taken for him,

1. The votes polled for him in such first-named constituency.

2. Then the votes polled for him in the second and third named and other following constituencies, for which he has offered himself consecutively.

3. Then the votes polled for him in the remainder of the constituencies in the order of their geographical proximity by their alphabetical order.

These rules give effect to all local attachments and influences, or real or supposed local interests,—a disregard of which attachments and influences is popularly supposed to be one of the inherent defects of Mr. Hare's plan. After the voting papers are liberated from the claims of one candidate as his quota is completed, and thus becomes a vote for the next candidate who is mentioned upon them, and being appropriated to him go to make up his quota, and after a certain number of quotas are thus made up, and candidates by these means declared elected for respective seats, we arrive at a point where there will be no full quota for any candidate by reason of a scattering vote, and yet the number necessary to fill the legislative chamber be incomplete. As we have divided the number of votes by the number of seats of the house, this result is inevitable, as the whole number of voters never vote, and there will be always, under the system supposed, a large scattering vote. A certain number of members—a number which may amount to one-half of the seats in the legislative hall—would therefore, under this system, have to be filled by men not having the full quotas or numbers of first choices after the process of cancellation has taken place. Mr. Hare gets over this difficulty in the following manner: By a process which he terms that of selection, he fills the legislative chamber with those having the largest number of first votes, pursuing throughout the course as though the candidate not having the full quota were in the same position as though he had such quota until the house is filled, beginning with the candidate having the highest number, and finishing the selection when the seats in the representative chamber are filled, though the last person selected has but half the number of votes necessary for a full quota.

If we suppose nothing more than the most ordinary degree of acquaintance with the names of a few public men, or even of one, coupled with that degree of interest in public affairs which would induce the voter to be at the pains of exercising his franchise, it is possible, and not even unlikely, that every voter in the country who may take the trouble to vote will be represented by a candidate whom he has especially named and selected. By fixing on any candidate of high and general reputation, the voter will be morally certain of securing him, if no other, as his representative in the national councils; and where the voter does not rely exclusively on one name, but introduces different names as so many alternatives, the system affords a practical application of that principle of compromise, the adaptation of the will, the pretensions, and the conduct to circumstances,—the yielding something of which we are less tenacious to secure for that on which we set a still higher value,—which is of such important influence and incalculable value in political as well as in social life. The voter expresses in effect his wish to be represented by the second person named on his paper if he cannot be by the first,—by the third if he cannot be by the second, and so on. Instead of crushing the opinions or sentiments of any voter, it leads him by a gentle and unresisted constraint to blend and harmonize them with those of others, until a voluntary unanimity is attained.

No occasion must be given for any doubt of the fidelity of the process of appropriation to the directions of the Electoral Law. Scarcely anything impairs more insidiously or fatally the public respect for a representative assembly, and the public confidence in it, than the suspicion that its seats have been filled by arts or contrivances which detract from its character as the true embodiment of the deliberate will of the nation. It will, therefore, be desirable to provide for a satisfactory verification by the public of the electoral result, and for a permanent record of it.

The general election officers shall, on the final appropriation of the voting papers, indorse on every voting paper the name of the candidate to whom it has been appropriated; and, after such indorsement shall have been made, the general election officers shall give all due facilities to candidates, agents, and others at their own cost for verifying the results of the poll and inspecting the voting papers; and such cost shall be settled by the general election officers, and shall not exceed the amount of the due remuneration of the clerks of the officers attending on such inspection; and the general election officers shall cause to be printed in a separate book for every member returned under their certificates, as aforesaid, the names of the voters whose voting papers have been appropriated to such member respectively, or number of ballots which he has, and copies of such a book shall be sold at a price not exceeding the rate at which the same cost the government; and, after sufficient time shall have been afforded for the purpose aforesaid, as well as gathering from the voting papers such statistical or other information as shall be thought useful, the general election officers shall cause all the voting papers to be redelivered to the several returning officers respectively from whom the same were received, and with whom they shall remain, and the same shall, with the voting papers set apart and retained by the returning officers, as aforesaid, be arranged in distinct volumes or files, every distinct volume or file containing the votes appropriated to one member or candidate only, and the votes within every volume or file shall be arranged alphabetically, according to the names of the voters; and on a copy of the list of the registered voters, opposite to every voter's name, shall be noted the number of the volume or file in which his voting paper is placed, and the same shall be at all reasonable times accessible to voters, candidates, and others requiring to inspect them, or any of them, at their own cost, and which cost shall be settled by the returning officers, and shall not exceed the due remuneration of the clerical labor and attention on such inspection, and every voter shall be at liberty to refer to and examine his own voting paper without cost.

The publication of separate books containing the method of appropriation will be calculated to afford satisfaction to the voter, while it will constantly tend to preserve the reality of the connection between the member and his constituents, and render it still more a matter of individual pride not to be unworthily represented.

It will be necessary to provide for the possibility of a candidate being elected by a sufficient number of voters to make up the quota, and who yet may not be in a position on the poll of any particular district to entitle him to require that the returning officer shall return him as elected by it. Suppose, for example, that there were five hundred different constituencies and a candidate had ten votes in every district, he might have the quota, or a comparative majority, but not a majority in any place. The supposed state of things is, of course, highly improbable; but there ought to be no possible defect in the operation of machinery designed to act perpetually and under all circumstances. If any cases should arise, such as has been supposed, it may be left to be dealt with by the house upon a form of proceeding which the candidate, or any of the electors interested, may be allowed to initiate.

When it shall appear by the certificate of the general election officers that any candidate has polled such a number of votes as shall amount to the quota, or to a comparative majority, and he shall not yet be returned by any returning officer as a member to serve in the representative body, and such candidate, or any of the voters by whom he has been chosen, shall present a petition to the representative body stating such facts, and praying that he may be admitted as the representative of such particular districts or voters, it shall be lawful for the representative body, upon hearing the said certificate of the general election officer, to declare by resolution that the said candidate has been duly elected as a member of the said house, and such declaration shall have the same effect as if he had been duly returned as a member by the returning officers.

Mr. Hare, from this stage on, carries his system to a degree of refinement unnecessary for practical purposes, and arrives at a point where the complexity is not counterbalanced by a corresponding utility.

To recapitulate the principles of this system:

(*a*) No vote to be counted for more than one candidate.

(*b*) No candidate to have more votes counted for him than the quota; *i.e.* the quotient of the whole number of persons voting, divided by the number of members to be returned for the legislative chamber for which the election is held. (Return by quotas.)

(*c*) Each voter to have the right of naming several candidates, in his order of preference, so that if his vote be not counted for the first on his list, it may have the chance of being counted for the second; if not for the second, then for the third, and so on. (Alternative voting.)

Thus are attained—

(1) *As regards the voter*, the power of expressing his approbation of a considerable number of candidates by naming them as successors to his vote without damaging the chances of those who stand highest in his preference. This power might perhaps be unlimited, or the number of names to be

placed on the card of any voter might be restricted to, say twenty, of the candidates about whom he would be likely to have some accurate knowledge, so as to exclude the adoption of long lists at mere party dictation.

(2) *As regards opinion or party*, the return, by any body of men acting in the same sense, of a number of members precisely proportioned to that of the quotas they made up, whether their acting in the same sense was concerted or resulted from their having, without consent, named candidates of similar opinions in their different voting districts.

(3) *As regards districts*, as each candidate runs for a particular geographical district, local preferences and interests are thus allowed their legitimate and proper play.

(4) *As regards the voter's range of choice*, a wide preference and number of candidates are given him, so that he may be able to express his approval, and assist in the return of one who might truly represent him, though none such were found among the local candidates.

(5) *As regards the representative*, if he be a man of pre-eminent ability, his position in the legislative chamber is no longer dependent upon a local majority, but upon the opinions formed of him by the whole country or State. His independence is thus secured, and political life becomes an honorable vocation, in which the best representative men of thought can engage with the certainty that their positions are not dependent upon the political jobbery of locality.

"The most malignant of the herd"
"In surest way to be preferred."

Mr. H. R. Droop, of London, one of the most earnest and intelligent of the many disciples of the principles of true representation, has kindly communicated to the author a modification of Hare's plan, based upon Mr. Walter Bailey's suggestions in his pamphlet on "Election of Representatives," which will go far to simplify the Hare system.

He says: "The mode of determining the electoral quotient under Mr. Hare's plan is to divide the number of valid votes by n, the number of representatives to be elected, and, neglecting the fraction if any, adopt the integral part of the result as the electoral quotient. I propose instead to divide the number of valid votes by $n \times 1$; that is, by the number of representatives increased by one, and to take for the electoral quotient the whole number next greater than the result of this division. With 5000 valid votes and 5 representatives to be elected, the electoral quotient, according to the ordinary method, will be 1000; according to my proposal it would be 834, as the result of dividing 10,000 by 6 is $833\frac{1}{3}$. So with 10,000 valid votes and 10 representatives the electoral quotient would be 910 instead of 1000, and with 20,000 valid votes and 20 representatives it would be 953 instead of 1000. In every case the adoption of this smaller electoral quotient will save a certain number of votes from being uselessly retained for candidates whose election is already secure. That my electoral quotient will always be sufficiently large is manifest from considering that, as the electoral quotient is necessarily greater than the result of dividing the total number of valid votes by $n + 1$, $n + 1$ times this electoral quotient must be greater than the total number of valid votes, and therefore it is impossible that $n + 1$ candidates should each obtain as many votes as the electoral quotient; in other words, any candidate who obtained my electoral quotient will necessarily be among the first n candidates. Thus, in the first example given above, if five candidates had 834 votes apiece there would be only 830 votes left for the sixth candidate.

"This smaller electoral quotient is only a practical recognition of the fact, that even with proportional representation there always may be a minority left without any direct representation.

"Where only one representative is to be elected, this minority may, as in a majority representation, be anything less than a half of the constituency; where there are two representatives it cannot exceed one-third; where there are five, it cannot exceed one-sixth; and where there are twenty, it cannot exceed one-twenty-first part; but it is impossible altogether to get rid of it. My second proposal, which may be adopted or rejected, independently of the first one, relates to the procedure to be adopted after all the votes have been drawn out of the urn, and the superfluous votes of the candidates who have already obtained sufficient votes have been distributed among the other candidates. The most usual procedure is simply to arrange the candidates who have not yet obtained the electoral quotient according to the number of votes each has obtained, and then take from the top of this list as many as are required to complete the number of representatives to be elected. M. Naville has lately, in the *Bibliothèque Universelle* for November, 1869, proposed another procedure in which he treats every voting paper not appropriated as part of the electoral quotient of a candidate already elected not only as a vote for the first candidate upon it, but also as a vote of smaller value for the second and every subsequent candidate upon it. The procedure I propose to adopt here is gradually to reduce the number of candidates to $n \times 1$, one more than the number of members to be elected, by always excluding from the competition the candidate who for the time has fewest first votes, and transferring each of his voting papers to the candidate next named upon it. There is evidently nothing unfair in this.

" The candidate who has fewest votes after all the superfluous votes have been distributed, cannot possibly be elected, and it is more merciful to him and his supporters to allow their votes to be transferred to some candidate with a better chance of success than to exclude them summarily from all influence in the election, as the procedure ordinarily proposed does. The principal object I have in view is to protect a party from the risk of losing its proportional share of the representation through too many candidates coming forward to represent it. Suppose, for instance, that five candidates come forward on behalf of a party whose numerical strength—say 3000 electors—only entitles it to three representatives. In such a case it may easily happen that, after the distribution of superfluous votes, the party finds that their votes are distributed somewhat after this fashion, 1000, 700, 600, 400, 300, so that the first three candidates have only 2300 votes between them instead of 3000, the other 700 votes being thrown away upon candidates who have no chance of being elected. If a rival party with only 2600 electors has only run three candidates, it will probably get three representatives, while the party with 3000 electors only gets two.

"According to my procedure the 700 votes should not be lost, but only transferred to the other candidates of the party, so that in the final contest for the odd number they would have all their 3000 votes to set against the 2600 of the rival party."

Mr. Hare discusses this proposal and pronounces against it: a plan for filling up casual vacancies had not then been proposed.

"The method of filling up vacancies, which has been proposed by the Neuchâtel Commission and by M. Naville, makes it important, not unnecessarily, to check the number of candidates brought forward by the same party. As the vacancies are to be filled up according to the votes given at the general election, out of the candidates not then elected, each party ought to be at liberty to bring forward additional candidates beyond the number of representatives its strength entitles it to, in order to replace any representatives of the party who may die or otherwise vacate their seats. It is desirable to guard against voting papers with only a few names of candidates upon them, being altogether lost, through not being drawn until after these candidates have obtained the quota. This may be done by providing that whenever a voting paper is drawn which only contains the names of candidates who have already obtained the quota, it shall be added to the votes of the first candidate named upon it, and instead of the last of the voting papers already appropriated to such candidate, which is capable of being transferred, shall be transferred to the first candidate named upon it who has not obtained the quota."

Mr. Droop, in a letter to the author, but recently received, gives an ingenious plan of marking the voting paper, so that the whole process of applying the votes may be checked and repeated by any one interested, and thus any fraud or mistake may be at once detected:

1393.

A		
B	2	~39~
C		
D	1	—
E	4	
F	3	379
G		

The voting paper is numbered 1393, in the order of its reception at the voting place. D, among the list of candidates, the first in order of preference by voter No. 1393, has already received his quota, and is therefore marked on third line of paper by a —. B, the voter's second choice, has the vote then assigned to him, which makes, say his 39th vote, and is so marked. After B's votes are distributed and it is found that not enough votes are cast for B to elect him, the number 39 is crossed, and F, the third choice,—but who has enough votes to elect him,—has the vote applied, which we will suppose, in that event, to be F's 379th vote, and is so marked. The voting paper, at the end of the process, will therefore stand as shown, and will tell the whole story of its application.

In the next chapter the other plans, to arrive at a proper system of representation, which have been suggested, will be considered.

CHAPTER V.

SAME SUBJECT CONTINUED.

In planning this chapter, many doubts arose to the author's mind whether it would be well to weary the general reader with the manifold reforms which have been suggested by different publicists to arrive at a more just carrying out of representative democracy. These doubts were dispelled, however, by the consciousness that, in writing a scientific treatise, we have no right to take into consideration the reader's frame of mind. First and foremost, we must acknowledge the great services which the Geneva reformers rendered, under the leadership of Ernest Naville, Roget, and Morin, to the cause of proportional representation. The *Association Réformiste* of that city have kept alive the discussion upon this subject throughout Switzerland, and, by means of their journal, "*La Réformiste,*" and numerous other publications, have carried the ideas of electoral reform far beyond the limits of their own country. The plan which they propose may be called the *independent ticket* voting. I prefer that name to *list voting*, the one given by Mr. D. D. Field[*] to this

---

[*] Proportional Representation, Putnam's Magazine, June, 1870.

scheme, as the French word *liste* has, in politics, its equivalent by our word "ticket." Any ticket of candidates, signed by thirty voters, and to contain the full number of candidates to be elected, may be deposited some certain time before the day of election in the hands of the president of elections. Each list, or ticket, receives a designated letter or number, and may, at the option of the voters who so deposit it, receive any other distinctive sign or appellation.

On the day of election, the voters vote for the full list of candidates upon the respective tickets by simply designating by letter or number the list of candidates to which they desire to have their votes applied.

The division of the number of votes cast at the election by the number of representatives to be elected gives the quotient necessary for the election of a deputy. The quantity of electoral quotients which any ticket obtains is the number of representatives to which such ticket is entitled, in the order of preference, printed or written upon it.

Let us take the case of Geneva, which elects forty-four deputies, and has about 4600 voters; the election might stand as follows:

Tickets.	Votes cast.	Deputies.
A	1943	19
B	1443	14
C	797	8
D	311	3
E	39	0
Scattering	27	0
	4560	44

To take an example nearer home, the plan in a congressional election for New York State would operate thus: The State of New York has, say 800,000 votes, and is to elect thirty-one congressmen, and the electoral quotient would be therefore 25,806 votes. As all voters do not vote, we might put the electoral quotient at 25,000. The result of an election under the Geneva plan might result as follows:

Tickets.	Votes.	Representatives.
Republicans. (Ticket A.)	250,000	10
Democrats. (Ticket B.)	275,000	11
Free-Traders. (Ticket C.)	75,000	3
Protectionists. (Ticket D.)	50,000	2
Civil Service Reformers. (Ticket E.)	50,000	2
Anti-Chinese candidates. (Ticket F.)	50,000	2
Fenian candidates. (Ticket G.)	25,000	1
	775,000	31

The election, disregarding fractions of full quotas, would therefore result in electing the first 10 names of the Republican ticket, the first 11 of the Democratic ticket, the first 3 of the Free-Trade ticket, etc. Should any vacancy occur after the election, by death or otherwise, the name next on the ticket on which the person was elected, whose seat is vacated, shall fill the vacancy. Should any representative be elected on more than one ticket, he shall be deemed elected for the ticket having the larger number of votes, and the vacancy in the other ticket or tickets be made up by the following name or names.*

Mr. J. Francis Fisher, of Philadelphia, in his admirable essay,† proposes for *municipal elections* a plan in all respects similar to the one of the Geneva reformers. This plan has many advantages over that of Mr. Hare, by reason of its simplicity, and some disadvantages, by reason of the full ticket system, which makes party action and party machinery a necessity, though it strips parties of much of their power for mischief by granting a proportional share of power to any respectable number of "bolters" from the regular organization. It is the simplest of the preferential voting systems. In Switzerland, however, parties have not acquired the mischievous strength that they have with us, and legislative corruption is all but unknown. A recent reform introduced into that country makes legislative representative reform of less importance than it is here. Each fiscal measure must, in some of the cantons, by means of the *facultative référendum*, be referred to

---

* Réforme du Système Electoral. Geneva, 1865.
† Reform of Municipal Elections. Philadelphia, 1866.

the people for adoption, and as the people can, without the intervention of the representative body, initiate and make new laws, the composition of the representative chamber becomes there of minor importance.

This *référendum* has been introduced into the greater number of the cantons, and works admirably. What would have become of the so-called "Land Grabs" if the people had been permitted to vote upon them before they became law? The agitation of these two reforms in Switzerland with such earnestness that the *référendum* has been adopted in a majority of the cantons, and the independent ticket plan of totality or personal representation of the Geneva reformers defeated by the Grand Council of Neuchâtel by a small majority of twenty one votes, speaks well for the intelligence of the Swiss people, and augurs the permanence of free institutions there. Would that we were on the same highroad to a cure of the evils from which we suffer as that which Switzerland took as a preventive for the self-same political cancers!

"The simplicity, facility, and fairness of this scheme," says Mr. Fisher in the pamphlet referred to, advocating a plan similar to the one of the Geneva reformers, "appears to the writer unquestionable; and with this it seems possible to adopt to a certain extent Mr. Hare's idea of preference, for if each voter, on his own ticket, were to number the members as he preferred them, or approved their fitness, the order of the names might in this manner be changed or reversed, and any name on each list which obtained a majority of preference marks would replace another which wanted them. This would not only give a desirable opportunity for selection but a positive advantage to those whose character in the community stands highest."

Mr. Fisher is entitled to the very great merit of looking a little further ahead than almost all who have written upon this subject of personal representation, by providing a plan for legal nominations as well as a system of representation, which is left to the local class of corrupt politicians, because no legal organization is provided by means of which people meet to nominate officers.

"It is necessary," he says, "to make the party machinery amenable to public law, so that fraud and perjury in the party nominations would be as susceptible of investigation and as liable to punishment as those which might be perpetrated at the polls. Unless we can attain this, all our well concocted plans of checks and balances and minority representation will be fruitless." He suggests the following: "That a statute empower every fifty electors, previously ascertained, to appoint one representative, who may or may not be of their number, to meet in a convention with power or authorization to act for his constituents, being signed by all of them and certified by a notary public. Other representatives of a similar number, similarly certified, would unite with them according to their affinities; and whenever a number of deputies be combined to represent a sixth part of the whole body of electors for municipal offices, they may be empowered to organize a separate meeting for nominations. As it is believed that there never have, in any place, been more than four parties engaged in 'a single election, it is supposed that no body of citizens, comprising less than the sixth of the whole, would at any time organize into a separate party. Of course the most numerous parties would unite more delegates in proportion to their number."

The only objection to this plan is the necessity that one-sixth of the electors should be compelled to combine before a nomination can be effected. It seems to us that a much less number — say one-twentieth — would be all-sufficient, as the fact of the very small number of parties now taking the field, under our present majority-system of elections, is no criterion whatever to judge the condition of parties, or the people, when a totality or personal system of representation has been once introduced.

Analogous to the plan of the Geneva reformers and of Mr. Fisher is the system proposed in France by the Baron de Layre,* by double elections. The method is one suggested by the present French system of elections, by which a second election is held whenever a candidate does not obtain an absolute majority. He recognizes the electoral quotient, but obtains it by a division of the voters entitled to vote instead of those who have voted at the last election, thus raising the number of votes necessary to elect

---

* Les Minorités et le Suffrage Universel. Paris, Dentu, 1863.

a candidate, and declaring each person elected who shall obtain such quota, and having successive elections until all who can obtain full quotas are members, and then to fill the vacant seats by those having the highest number of votes. Another plan of total representation is one suggested by Maria Chenu in a pamphlet published about three years ago at Paris on the rights of minorities. It also involves a double election: the first to ascertain the relative strength of parties; after which an official assignment of representatives to each party in proportion to its strength, and then an election by majority in the parties themselves of the representatives for the legislative body.

Having at sufficient length explained the preferential plan of totality representation, we shall now proceed to examine the systems of *proxy voting*, which have the same object in view as the plans heretofore examined, but aim at its accomplishment by means of a somewhat different machinery: the first, in point of time which has been suggested, as it is in fact synchronal with the first edition of Mr. Hare's plan, is the one proposed by Mr. Fisher for the election of national representatives, in which he repudiates the general ticket and adopts what we have seen proper to call proxy voting. This plan, to use Mr. Fisher's own words,* is as follows:

1. As to the qualification of voters, whatever may be the provisions for this object, it is only necessary

---

* The Degradation of our Representative System and its Reform. Philadelphia, 1863.

that it should be such as to render probable the respectability of the voter and his interest in upholding the institutions of his country.

2. The secret vote, or ballot, must be abandoned.

3. The division of States into districts for election to the presidential or legislative offices must also be abandoned,—the least reflection showing that it is not land nor the owners of it who form our constituencies, but the citizens generally, and that the opinions, principles, and interests of the people, which ought really to find expression in their representatives, can never be expected to conform to any possible territorial division.

These questions being put aside, the framework and machinery of the new electoral system will be presented as briefly as possible.

I. In the first place, a registrar-general must be appointed in every State, with as many deputies in the different counties as may be necessary, with general and local offices of record.

II. The duty of the registrars should be to prepare a list of all the qualified voters in the State, dividing them according to the residences in townships or wards, and arranging their names alphabetically. This should be a permanent record of easy reference at the local and general registry offices.

III. Six months before each general election there should be a publication of all the qualified voters on record, the lists being printed in the local papers and exposed in various public places in every township or ward.

IV. After the publication, two or three months

should be given for additions or corrections, to be decided upon by the registrar; after which time no appeal should be heard, and the lists closed. The names of the additional voters, if any, should be published as above.

V. The registrar's books being closed, and the whole number of qualified voters being ascertained, the numerical constituency of each member of the national or State legislature may be determined by using as a divisor the number of places to be filled. But it is not necessary to count the whole number of qualified voters,—the largest number of votes given in any previous election, with a proportional addition for the estimated increase in population, may be taken as the aggregate; the quotient produced by the number of representatives as a divisor may be accepted as the whole constituency of each member, to be procured by the candidate in any part of the State.

VI. Immediately after closing the books of registry, a ticket should be furnished from the registrar's office to every qualified voter, stating his right to vote for each member of Congress or State legislature, or any other elective officer: a separate ticket for each office. The ticket might have some such form as the following:

"John Doe is authorized to vote for a member of Congress (or other office), of which this ticket is his certificate. An assignment by writing on the back is necessary to convey the vote to the member of his choice."

Signed by the registrar.

N. B.—This ticket should be numbered and prepared in such a way as to guard against counterfeit.

VII. The ticket thus placed in the hands of an elector is not to be used at an ordinary polling place, but regularly assigned to the representative before a notary public, or some similar officer,—the number and names being entered on a record kept for that purpose; and the tickets so assigned are to be handed to the member elect as his certificate, to be presented and counted at the proper office of the legislative body to which he is elected.

VIII. Several days (ten are proposed) should be allowed for this assignment previous to the closing of the election, and it might not be found objectionable for the notary to receive the assignment of a vote at the house of an elector in case of serious illness.

IX. No more votes would be required for or given to one candidate than the number making the complement of his constituency. Others, which might be offered, could be passed over by the advice of the member elect, or his committee of canvass, to some other candidate representing similar interests or principles.

X. As votes would coalesce in this manner, it is presumed that the greatest number of places in the legislative body would be filled by a totality vote. The few seats not receiving the full complement might be filled by those candidates whose number of votes exceeds two-thirds of what constitutes a perfect constituency; and if, in fine, in consequence of the great number of candidates, there should still be a seat unfilled, a new election might be declared, at which all the voting tickets not previously effective might be again used.

The objection to this plan of proxy voting is that the vote ceases to be a solemn act. It is accompanied by none of the forms which impress upon the citizen the fact that, in exercising the franchise, he performs a public trust, and does not merely indicate an individual predilection. The voting paper would have a marketable value, and would be bought up by candidates as men buy shares of stock or lottery tickets. Mr. Fisher may answer that, if people will sell their votes, and be misgoverned in consequence, there is nothing to be done but to raise their moral standard; and, in the second place, the class of men who would sell their votes will be the same as do so now. Our answer is, that the man who sells his vote not only injures himself, but every honest member of the community as well, and that this peculiar system of proxy voting gives special facilities for the sale or giving away of votes, as the act of transfer impresses upon the elector less the true fiduciary nature of the vote than the process of going to the polls.

There is another plan of proxy voting, which was sanctioned by the Personal Representation Society of New York, and was pressed by it upon the constitutional convention, which met in the State of New York in 1867, in a memorial prepared at the request of the society, by the author. It was seen fit to prepare a special plan, because none, except that of the Geneva reformers, seemed fully to meet the double requirements of justice and of simplicity. Hare's and the plans of the reformers herein referred to, meet them by returning to the true principle of representation, so that the people, as a whole, and not a part, are represented; but they all introduce, in the first place, the inequality of giving to persons having less than a quota of votes the same voice in legislation as to such who, by reason of their popularity, might have obtained a dozen quotas; and, in the second place, they create the difficulty that the voter's vote does not go where he wants it to be most effective, in case the man who is his first choice is elected before his voting paper under Hare's plan is counted, or gathered, as under Fisher's plan. Hare tells us that the voter's condition is bettered by reason of his first choice being already elected before his voting paper is counted,—as the man whom he wants, more especially, in the legislative chamber or halls of Congress is already elected, and he has a chance to add to the quota of some other friend of his political opinions. This is a specious statement of the case. In the first place, the voter may not have as full a confidence in any other man as in him whom he has placed at the head of his ticket, and may think, justly or mistakenly, that the success of any other person on the list of candidates would simply tend to hinder and clog the operations of the member whom he desires to see in the legislative body. Their schemes also fail to give proper force to the fact that, as Mr. Fisher says himself; "the greater part of the people, devoted as they are to their respective occupations, cannot, and will not, devote the time necessary to canvass the merits of all the candidates who present themselves for the suffrages of their fellow-citizens. Among the educated the real choices would be exhausted in the second or third line of the voting paper, and the rest of the names of candidates, if placed there at all, would be there by the mere dictates of chance or caprice."

We must also consider that all public duties, such as voting, sitting on juries, etc., are, more or less, shirked by all but the most public-spirited of our citizens, and those who have a direct interest in their performance. Any substitute for the single vote by the preferential vote, or any other complex plan, would result, therefore, in a very great immediate diminution of the percentage of votes cast. It is to be feared that, with the great mass, the case will stand still worse: the first choice would exhaust their volition, and the other and subsequent choices would be placed upon the ticket at the dictate of a demagogue, or of parties.

The obstacles in the way of the people meeting in assembly and originating their own measures of legislation and government are, as before observed, their number and their distance from each other. They must, therefore, deliberate and cast their votes through their accredited agents. For one of the reasons mentioned, these agents should not be too numerous, and we must, therefore, put a minimum limit to the number of powers of attorney that any candidate must hold before he is entitled to a seat in the legislative body. Such provisions would prevent too numerous a body. The State of New York has about 800,000 voters. If it be desirable to have no more than the number of members which compose the present assembly, by dividing the number of votes by 128, the number of seats, we have a quotient of a trifle over 6000 votes as quota to elect a representative as the minimum number of proxies or powers of attorney (votes) necessary to entitle a candidate to a seat. In using the word proxies, or powers of attorney, we do not mean that the candidates shall actually procure a certain number of powers of attorney, made out in due form, but to express our meaning of the legal and logical significance of a vote, each vote being regarded as a power of attorney. Every person receiving, at any election for members of assembly, a larger number of votes than the minimum quota fixed by law, should be deemed elected, and each member give, in the legislative body upon every measure or act coming to a vote, either one vote for every thousand votes which have been cast for him, or the number of ballots cast for him, and which he represents, be they six thousand or twenty thousand.

To obviate the objection, if it be thought to have any force, that the plan proposed might result in giving us too few members of the assembly by the concentration of a great number of votes upon a few popular men, the State might be divided into assembly districts sufficiently large to give the fullest expression to the then prevalent popular opinions, and restrict the choice of votes to candidates residing in such districts. The people then, in point of fact, would, upon every measure, vote through their agents, the representatives, as though they were owners of shares of stock in a railroad or mining corporation, and with like effect.

The objections to this plan would be as follows:

Under this plan, one member may have in the legislative chambers ten times as much power as some other member. Of course, and why should he not have if he represents ten times more of the power-giving element than another?

Another objection would be that under this system the legislative body would not consist of any fixed number; it may be one hundred and twenty-eight persons this year, and but twenty the next. To which we answer:

Why should it consist of a fixed number after we have provided against the dangers of having our representative body too large for business, or too small for deliberative purposes, by means of the minimum quota of votes which each member is to represent, and the division of the State into large electoral districts? If the voters of the State of New York desire to be represented, and believe that they are best represented by having but twenty representatives to cast all their votes upon the legislative acts, why should the people not be gratified? That contingency is, however, not likely to take place. A man must be very popular, indeed, to be able to control one-twentieth of all the votes of the State in opposition to the competition of all those candidates who would be satisfied with just sufficient votes to entitle them to seats in the assembly. If, however, it be thought advisable to have an assembly with a determined number of members, then it may be provided, that such of the number, after those having one or more quotas are declared elected, necessary to fill the legislative body who have the highest number of votes up to the quota shall be permitted to hold the unfilled seats. Casting, however, only the number of votes, or partial quotas they respectively represent, and no more, as, under this plan, there would still be a small fraction of voters unprovided for by representatives, by reason of their votes being scattered upon such candidates as have not even received approximate minimum quotas, which could easily, without much injustice, be left unprovided for and unrepresented, or what, to our mind, would be more correct, as we do not believe in disfranchising a man because he has not succeeded in electing his candidate to office, it might be provided that every citizen having voted for a person who is not elected, and who, therefore, cannot cast the voter's vote on public questions in the legislature, shall have the right to transfer his vote, within one week after the election, to any one of the successful candidates. In this way, again, every vote in the community would actually be represented in the representative body.

Of course, this right to transfer must be reserved only for those who voted for unsuccessful candidates, and thereby run the risk of becoming disfranchised; or, the unsuccessful candidates might be constituted into an electoral body to meet within a short period after the election, and, by some public and legal manner, either transfer their votes to the successful candidates, or add to each other's quota, until some of their number have sufficient votes to entitle them to seats.

An ingenious objection to this plan, which struck the author at first blush with much force, is one which was urged in a letter received by him from Walter Morrison, Esq., M. P., one of the best of men, and one of the strongest advocates for reform in the direction of personal representation both in and outside of the English Parliament. He says that the popular man who has been elected on one issue by half a dozen quotas, and therefore holds half a dozen votes in the legislative chamber, would wield the same power on some question upon which he had not been elected, and as to which the greater part of his constituents may be opposed to him. For instance, a representative elected upon the question of free trade, with six quotas, might cast those votes upon a resolution tending to embroil us with a foreign power, when the feeling in his constituency might be opposed to him utterly on that very question. The objection, however, has but little practical weight. Popular men are those who keep in the current of popular opinion, and they are generally but too willing to sacrifice their convictions of right to the desire to retain their popularity, and are therefore sure to keep themselves well posted as to what opinion is the more prevalent. And the objection urged by Mr. Morrison may be entirely obviated, if, by the substitution of the open vote for the ballot and the registering of the vote we allow each person who voted for any particular candidate to withdraw his vote during the session of the legislative body from such candidate, and thus give the people the right not only to withdraw power from the candidate, but also leads to this result: that if the withdrawal of votes leaves the representative without a full quota, it shall operate as a recall from his position.

This power should be guarded from abuse by a proviso that the people, who voted for a candidate they see proper to recall, should not be permitted to be represented in any form during the session of the legislative body, as otherwise there would be endless agitation by political aspirants for the purpose of profiting by the recall of political incumbents.

We now come to the examination of the two plans which may in strictness be called, in contradistinction to the totality or personal schemes, the minority plans of representation. These are the cumulative and limited plans of voting.

The *cumulative plan* is the one which has been very ably urged by Senator Buckalew, of Pennsylvania, and, mainly through the influence of the *Chicago Tribune*, has been adopted in the Constitution of the State of Illinois, which is to go into operation in 1872.

By this plan each voter has the right to cast as many votes as there are representatives to be elected, and he may concentrate his votes upon one of the candidates, or divide them up as he may see fit. According to the Illinois provision, each district sends three instead of one representative, and each voter can concentrate his votes upon one, or distribute them between the three. A minority, having one-third or more of the voters, can therefore always, by the concentration of all their votes upon one candidate, secure his election.

This plan was proposed to the Senate of the United States in a report by Senator Buckalew, in which he, after eloquently inveighing against the evils of the present system, recommended the cumulative plan of voting as their cure. And last June the same plan was brought forward by Mr. S. S. Marshall, one of the members from Illinois, in the House of Representatives, and supported by him in a convincing and thoroughly able speech. The question came up on the apportionment of representatives under the census of 1870, the Senate having enacted that the number of representatives under the new census shall be limited to 300 instead of 244 members, and apportioned among the States in accordance with their population.

Mr. Marshall proposed as an amendment, or additional section, the following:

"*Be it further enacted*, That, in all cases at any election where there shall be two or more members of Congress elected in any State by general ticket, each qualified voter at such election may cast as many votes for one candidate as there are representatives to be thus elected, or may distribute the same, or equal parts thereof, among the candidates, as he shall see fit, and the candidates highest in votes shall be declared elected."

Much to the surprise of Mr. Marshall himself, he found support in Mr. S. S. Cox, of New York, Mr. Haldeman, of Pennsylvania, and Mr. Garfield, of Ohio, and almost carried the house with him upon a question which must have been a new one to the great majority of the members of the House of Representatives.*

If we make the districts large enough to comprise the whole State, and thus give, by the cumulative plan, a representative to any small minority in the community, there can be no opposition to the plan proposed, except its cumbersomeness; but with small districts electing but three members it has the disadvantage that, while it gives to the minority (always provided that it be one-third and more of all voters of the district) one representative, it does not get rid of, but on the contrary makes permanent, party action and party machinery, and in making a nomination equivalent to an election, removes the corruption from the election to the nominating conventions. The residents of New York have seen such a plan work very badly in the election of their boards of supervisors,—the results as to men selected we need not comment upon; and the bad working of this scheme will be laid to the door of the system of totality or personal representation, recommended by those who are designated *doctrinaires* by such who call themselves practical, because they contemn principles, and believe the incorporation of a grain of truth with a

---

* Daily Globe, Friday, June 24, 1870.

mass of error to be better than the securing of the whole of a truth. The evil which the cumulative plan, coupled with the small districts, utterly fails to reach, is the permanent division of the country into majorities and minorities; and we have already shown that that division is an unnatural one, and due entirely to the fact that our system of representation is partial and not complete.

The remaining plan which we have to consider is the *limited* voting. This plan has obtained prominence because a clause in the English reform bill of 1867 and 1868 was therein incorporated, on the motion of Lord Cairns, in the House of Lords, by virtue of which in what are called "the three-cornered constituencies" —*i.e.* those constituencies which return three members to Parliament—the voter is permitted to vote for but two, thus also enabling the minority to return one member. Lord Cairns foresaw that England was drifting toward manhood suffrage, and he desired thus to secure to the minority of the instructed class of Englishmen some chance to be heard, when the whole people, the majority of whom in all communities are uninstructed, or, at best, but partially educated, shall hold, under a majority system, absolute sway. It was conceded even by those members of Parliament who are in favor of minority representation that the plan did not give full satisfaction; yet on the motion of Mr. Hardcastle for the repeal of that clause made in the last session of Parliament,* Mr. Hardcastle had in his favor the

---

* The Times (London), Thursday, June 16, 1870.

powerful support of Mr. Gladstone, and the indirect influence of Mr. Bright, the latter of whom is opposed, for reasons we know not, to minority representation: it is charitable, however, to assume that it is because he does not understand the subject. The arguments in favor of the retention of the minority clause made by Mr. Walter Morrison, the member for Plymouth, and Mr. Fawcett, the member for Brighton, were so irresistible that the motion for repeal was defeated by a majority of eight, and the *London Times* of the day following, in commenting upon this vote, said:

"The vote of yesterday confirmed the principle of representing minorities, and, as we believe, forever. The clauses in the reform act of 1867 were novelties which vehemently offended many democratic instincts, and great efforts were made at the general election to pledge Liberal candidates to vote for their repeal. The attempt has failed, and the passion which stimulated it has already lost much of its force, and will continuously diminish until it disappears. Time will establish the true principle more and more firmly in the reason and judgment of the nation. It cannot have escaped observation, though we make the remark with reluctance, that the opposition to it is found chiefly among the elder generation of the political world; and it is certain that some score of years hence, when the men of that time shall be fighting in defense of the novelties of their day, they will point their arguments by referring to the extraordinary fact that, when it was first sought to engraft a method of representing minorities upon the previous electoral methods, the proposal was opposed by the leaders of both the great parties of the State. By that time the principle will be so thoroughly accepted as axiomatic in all free countries that the reference may not improbably be received with incredulity. Mr. Morrison showed yesterday how quickly and widely it has spread since it was formally sanctioned by Parliament in 1867. Canton after canton of Switzerland, State after State of America, have taken it up, the last fact being the nearly unanimous promulgation of a proposition by the constitutional convention of Illinois that that foremost State of the Union shall be divided into three-cornered constituencies, with the cumulative vote in each. The principle has in truth within itself the conditions of its own success. Those who fight against it fight against light." *

The objection to that minority scheme, which we may now regard as part of the British Constitution, is of the same character as the one which we urged against the cumulative plan. It is not broad enough. It does not fully represent the people; it simply aims at and accomplishes the representation of powerful minorities in large districts: but, in recognizing the principle of minority representation, a step in the right direction has been taken which will open the way for a better and truer plan of representative governments.

The judiciary clause of the Constitution of New

---

* London Times, June 16, 1870.

York, in the election for judges of the court of appeals, adopts this limited system of voting by providing that the election shall be by general ticket for the whole State, and that each ticket shall contain the names of but five candidates; as there were seven to be elected, the minority party obtained two of the judges.

Shortly after the vote which took place in Parliament on Mr. Hardcastle's motion, the Elementary Education Act was passed by a very large majority, and in this act the government introduced a clause giving to electors of school-boards throughout the kingdom the cumulative vote.

The London Representative Reform Association, in their last report, say: "This recognition of the propriety and justice of the principle, that, in forming elective bodies for the difficult and important work of national education, they should represent every considerable section of opinion, instead of being the mere creatures of local majorities, is of great significance. As the public attention is awakened to this partial application of the principle, it will become more difficult to resist the conclusion that it ought to be extended to the constitution of the governing bodies, to which the determination of other great political and social questions is intrusted."*

A very significant fact, and one of which the educational influence is of the very highest impor-

---

* Report of the Representative Reform Association, 1870. London: 9 Buckingham Street, Strand.

tance is, that Harvard University has seen fit, under the advice and influence of Mr. Ware, to adopt a modification of Mr. Hare's scheme in the election of the board of trustees of the college. The four rules which embody this scheme are as follows:

I. Every candidate receiving one-tenth of the number of ballots cast to be nominated.

II. Each elector to send in the names of any number of candidates all on one ballot, indicating his preference among them by placing the figure 1 against the name of his first choice, 2 against that of his second choice, and so on.

III. Each ballot will be counted for the first choice indicated upon it alone, the other names being considered as substitutes, to be resorted to in the order of the preference indicated. Only in case the person named as the first choice has enough votes to nominate him without it, or in case he has not enough votes to entitle him to a nomination.

IV. The ballots will be counted in the order in which they are received.

The plan adopted by Harvard College resembles not only that of Mr. Hare, but is closely analogous to the system under which all elections are held for membership of the Rigsraad in Denmark, since 1855. We have refrained from drawing attention to this fact before, because, after we have convinced the reason of our reader that representation, by some such plan as we have explained, is just and right, the important practical questions will spring to his mind, Will it work? And what may be the result of its working? To answer these questions we shall quote largely from a Report made by the Rt. Hon. Robert Lytton, Secretary of the English Legation at Copenhagen, dated July 1, 1863, in answer to instructions of Lords Clarendon and Russell, in 1857 and 1860.*

The electoral law, the practical working of which is explained by Mr. Lytton, is one which was devised by Mr. Andræ, Ex-Minister of Finance of Denmark. In giving the history of representative legislation in that kingdom, this report says:

"The constitutional history of Denmark, although comparatively short, is far from deficient in interesting phenomena. Nurseries of self-government were planted in this country in 1834 by Frederick VI., who then established Consultative States throughout the kingdom; so that when, after the revolutionary movement which convulsed Europe in 1848, it was deemed advisable to expand the basis of government in this country, the population was not wholly unprepared for increased participation in the management of public affairs. Those, indeed, who at that period were engaged in the work of political reconstruction appear to have been disposed to give to the representative element a larger scope than was eventually accorded to it, and they justified their hesitation on the ground that the constituencies were as yet too inexperienced. An able writer, who has warmly engaged in the defense of Mr. Andræ's electoral system, has ridiculed this notion by pointing out that the greater the electioneering ex-

---

* Published by Henderson, Rait & Fenton. London, 1867.

perience of the constituency (that is to say, the more *rusés* the electors), the more certainly must the majority (unless some provision exist to the contrary) succeed in crushing the minority and monopolizing power. For if, as would have been the case under the system then contemplated, 65 members were to be chosen by 65,000 electors, no one elector being entitled to increase the value of his vote by voting for less than the full number of candidates, it is clear that the majority, consisting of 32,501 electors, would only have to hold firmly together in order to carry the whole number of the 65 seats in accordance with their choice. And in that case, no matter how prudently or sagaciously the minority, consisting of 32,499 electors, might exercise their franchise, these 32,499 electors would remain without any representative at all. How, then, should the real opinions of the electors be ascertained, in order that they may be represented in their just proportion? Suppose that of these 65,000 electors, a compact majority of 32,501 is opposed to various dispersed minorities, amounting altogether to 32,499. If the elections are distributed over 65 districts, it is possible that 32,064 of the majority might be found united in 64 districts against 31,936 of the minority. So that it would be only in the 65th district that the minority could make its voice heard. Nevertheless, the majority could only, with strict justice, claim 33 seats, and the remaining 32 should, in that case, it is clear, fall to the representation of various opinions, provided those opinions be not so dispersed as to be unable to come together in any place.

"To attain this result—to secure the adequate representation of every tangible opinion and corporate interest, in such way that, while the majority of the electors shall be able to name the majority of the representatives, the minority of the electors shall be insured an equivalent minority in the representation—this is the great problem which, in 1855, Mr. Andræ undertook to solve.

"Of all men in this country, his Excellency was, in many respects, the most fitted, by antecedent experience and natural qualifications, to succeed in the difficult task which he thus spontaneously attempted.

"Mr. Andræ is a man of original and speculative intellect, a keen investigator, a bold thinker, admitted by all his countrymen to be the first mathematician in Denmark, and, from his position as Minister of Finance, experienced in the art of bringing the fundamental principles of abstract calculation practically to bear upon complicated facts.

"The scope of his experiment, however, was painfully limited by conditions over which he had no control; and the law of which he is the sole author forms only the incidental part of an institution shaped rather by the force of uncongenial circumstances than by the deliberate option of the ostensible founders of it."

The uncongenial circumstances here referred to by Mr. Lytton were the existence, as independent autonomies, of the Duchies, which Germany has since wrested from Denmark. These Duchies had an electoral system of their own, which could not be interfered with. Mr. Lytton, after showing the composition of the Rigsraad, so far as the Duchies are concerned, says:

"The composition of the Rigsraad is, therefore, threefold,—20 members being nominated by the crown, 30 indirectly, and 30 directly elected; in all, 80 members.

"According to the census of 1860, the entire population of the kingdom and Duchies amounted to 2,604,024, so that it was only for the direct election of 30 members out of a population of upwards of 2,000,000 to an assembly of 80 members that the electoral system of Mr. Andræ was empowered to provide. Holstein and Lauenburg have always refused to send members to the Rigsraad. For these Duchies the constitution of 1855 is suspended, and therefore 20 members must be deducted from the total of 80 nominally composing the Rigsraad, and 8 members from the 30 originally contemplated as the quota of direct representation in the Rigsraad; consequently it is only the choice of 45 out of 60 members that is practically affected by the electoral system of Mr. Andræ.

"This, no doubt, diminishes the value to be attached to the success or failure of the system as an example. It is somewhat like an experiment in a pond upon principles of navigation, which, if good for anything, must be good for the ocean. Nevertheless, it is an example, and, in questions of this sort, an example of any kind is most valuable. Eight years' practical experience of the working of an electoral system devised for the realization of an important principle, applicable to all representative institutions, is—no matter how 'cabined, cribbed, confined' be the sphere of that experience—a great and noteworthy addition to the knowledge of mankind.

"Under circumstances so disheartening and within limits so restricted as those already mentioned, a mere perfunctory legislator might well have shrunk from the thankless task of pondering first principles in a matter of secondary effect. It would have been easy to have left untouched the root of a difficulty by which nobody was at that time greatly alarmed.

"But Mr. Andræ seems to have thought that no question affecting the duty of individuals and the welfare of nations can, under any circumstances, be of secondary importance; that superficial legislation, even on a small scale, is a great evil, and the political embodiment of a right principle, however minute, a great good.

"Nay, the very circumstances which limited the number and reduced the influence of the direct representatives of the nation in the national legislature, rendered it doubly important that these representatives should, at least, be the very best.

"If the voice of the constituencies was only to weigh in a scale of less than one to two among the voices composing the supreme council of the realm, it was all the more incumbent upon the state to provide that the true opinions and interest of those constituencies should be accurately expressed by men of the highest intelligence and character.

"But this was not the only good which it was

possible to attain, and therefore necessary to attempt. By bringing into view a higher standard of representative intelligence, to raise in the sequel the moral and intellectual standard of the constituencies themselves,—to impress, as much as might be, on the mind of every voter that he is called by the state to the performance of a solemn duty, not merely indulged in the enjoyment of a noisy right,—to constrain him to reflect and select,—to induce him to think calmly, and enable him to feel rightly, by extricating him as much as possible from narrowing and ignoble influences,—this, also, was an object to be striven for, inasmuch as the character of nations is but the collective expression of the character of individuals, and the political greatness of the one must, in the long run, depend upon the moral and intellectual worth of the other. Especially is this the case with those states in which the form of government is popular. In popular states, says Montesquieu, a force other and greater than the constraining power of the laws, or the arm of the prince, is needed for self-preservation: '*cette force c'est la vertu.*'

"To effect such a result it was foreseen that it would be necessary not indeed to dislocalize entirely the sympathies and associations of the voter, but by the removal of arbitrary restrictions to expand the range and elevate the character of his choice.

"The various clauses of the Electoral Law of 1855 sufficiently indicate, I think, that, although the conclusions of its author were no doubt arrived at by a mathematical process, these political considerations were not absent from his mind.

"It was not possible to obliterate entirely the old electoral divisions. But these were simplified and rearranged by expanding the area, and reducing the number of them. The great object in view, however, was to secure to each elector a reasonable certainty that his vote should bear its full value in favor not of some candidate imposed upon his adoption by local restrictions and local caucuses, but of the candidate really preferred by him in the free exercise of his individual judgment; and it was felt that this object was to be attained rather by a just electoral basis than by any merely geographical arrangement. To find such an electoral basis was the real problem. 'You will find it,' said Mr. Andræ, 'if you divide the number of electors by the number of members to be elected, and take the quotient as the quota of votes necessary and sufficient for the election of each candidate. This is the only just electoral basis.'"

Mr. Lytton then proceeds to set forth the sections of the law which prescribe the preferential plan. It is so much like that of Mr. Hare that we shall not encumber the text with it, but append it as a guide for practical legislation. After explaining the advantages of the law and the reasons thereof, with which our reader must be by this time familiar, he concludes as follows:

"To sum up the result of the foregoing inquiry into the mechanical operation of the Electoral Law of 1855, it appears, firstly, that the most ingenious and elaborately devised combination of objections to the electoral mechanism of Mr. Andræ's system is fixed upon two postulates,—the one political, the other mathematical,—of which the first is preposterous and the second impossible. Secondly, that the utmost ingenuity of artifice is only able to erect upon a basis, thus enormous in its unsubstantiality, an hypothesis minute in its material import of injustice to a single candidate out of three—in a single district out of all. Can as much be affirmed of any other existing electoral system?

"In this report, which has already, I fear, greatly exceeded its legitimate limits, no more need be said as to the practicability of the law and the accuracy of its mechanical operation.

"Other, and perhaps yet more important, considerations, however, are involved in the questions of what are its political results in this country, and how far it may be applicable to other European communities.

"I may mention, however, that, on lately referring to some of these topics in conversation with a Danish gentleman well acquainted with the political life of this country, I was assured that, in the discussion and settlement of great public questions by the supreme council of the realm, no disinclination is found to exist upon the part of representative minorities to combine and concur in the formation of a judicial majority for the decision of what is expedient.

"I may also mention that I have been assured by Mr. Andræ that, in his opinion, the general standard of representative character supplied by this law is the best and highest in the country; and that, although he does not consider that a sufficient time has yet elapsed whereby to test the effects of the law upon the constituencies themselves, he is, nevertheless, of opinion that, under its operation, the character of the voter as a class has improved and is improving. I have every reason to believe, moreover, that bribery is almost unknown to the constituencies for the Rigsraad.

"A full and complete investigation into the character and operation of this law is a task which I should rejoice to see assumed by some person of known impartiality, capacity, and experience. For, whatever may be the character or the consequence of the law, I venture to think that its existence is one-of the most remarkable events in the history of representative institutions.

"There is a saying of Lord Coke's, repeated by Junius, in reference to a matter of some importance in our own parliamentary history, that 'discretion, taken as it ought to be, is *discernere per legem quid sit justum.*' "

As to the question whether or not such a plan can work in practice, we answer that it has worked for fifteen years in Denmark, and it would not be consonant with our national pride to admit that the Danes are capable of a more intelligent exercise of the suffrage than Americans, and that that which is not too complex for them to practice is too complex for us to understand.

CHAPTER VI.

OTHER SUGGESTIONS FOR REFORM.

It is due to the thinkers who have respectively proposed reforms of evils inherent in democratic institutions not depending upon the idea of totality representation to pass their plans in review. Among such Robert Von Mohl and John Stuart Mill are perhaps the most eminent. In the work on Constitutional and International Law and Politics,* Mohl, after reviewing the different methods of constituting the representative body, as the appointing by the sovereign, by right of birth, by elections by the people, or a part thereof, and indicating the evils to which they are incident, lays down as indispensable for the formation of a good representative body the following conditions:

A. The members should possess a thorough understanding of the rights and interests which they represent, and be zealous in their support.

B. The choice of members fulfilling these conditions should not be left to the operations of chance, but measures should be taken to make the probability almost a certainty that such only will be elected.

---

* Tübingen, 1860, vol. i. p. 367, etc.

C. This probability does not exist unless the candidature is restricted to such men only, who have immediate and direct relations to the rights and interests which they are called upon to represent. Thus alone can duty and pleasure be reconciled and combined with special and technical knowledge. We mistake human nature in supposing that a sense of duty, a statesmanlike insight, personal ambition, or a regard for public opinion, will prove as efficient a motive as personal interest.

D. Then we must not forget that the rights and interests of a nation which are to be protected and defended are of three kinds: 1st, general interests; 2d, special interests, as pertaining to groups; and 3d, individual interests. The representative body should be so constituted that these threefold factors be not intermingled nor mistaken, but held in view, and by their counteraction and repercussion hold each in its proper sphere.

E. Representation should be proportional; that is to say, the number of members ascribed to each interest should be in accordance with its importance.

F. To obtain this result, there should be three representative bodies: the first representing the individual, the second the class, and the third the general interests. The third body should be selected by the other two, and have a veto upon their measures; thus, in the first or lowest representative body, the so-called popular men—men who talk well, who gain a large circle of friends, but who do not represent any special class-interest or ideas—would find their place. The second would be representative of the aristocratic, landed, mercantile, banking, manufacturing, and agricultural interests of the State, also all subdivisions of these interests; and thus by Mohl's plan one great good would be attained, that legislators of class-interests would be known, and could not, under the guise of patriotism or appeals to popular prejudices and fallacies, benefit by legislation the class that elected them. The representative of the wool-growers or woolen manufacturers would make his argument for the interest by which he is retained, and would not and could not pretend that it is for the interest of the whole country that he contends.

In the third chamber such only who have risen intellectually above the narrow circle of personal popularity, and the restricted anti-social ideas of class, would properly find their places. The statesmen, the political economists, and eminent publicists — the men who have devoted their lives to questions of international law and jurisprudence — would in that event guide the nation and hold all individual and class legislation in check. How far it is possible to put in practice this very symmetrical system of Mohl is a difficult question to determine. That the three classes of interests exist in every developed social organism is a fact which does not admit of controversy, and that under our present organization we, in an incomplete sort of way, succeed in representing them, is also true; but the difficulty, as Mohl happily puts it, is that they are not kept separate and distinct in the minds of the people, and thus the lower interests have always foisted themselves upon us under the guise of general interests.

Mr. Mill lays much stress upon the necessity of weighing as well as counting votes. After advocating the extension of the suffrage to all men who are not receiving parish relief, or who are not criminals, uncertificated bankrupts, idiots, etc., he says:* "Yet, in this state of things the great majority of voters in most countries, and emphatically in this, would be manual laborers, and the twofold dangers, that of too low a standard of political intelligence and that of class legislation, would still exist in a very perilous degree. It remains to be seen whether any means exist by which these evils can be obviated.

"They are capable of being obviated if men sincerely wish it, not by any artificial contrivance, but by carrying out the natural order of human life, which recommends itself to every one in things in which he has no interest or traditional opinion running counter to it.

"In all human affairs, every person not directly interested and not under positive tutelage, has an admitted claim to a voice, and, when his exercise of it is not inconsistent with the safety of the whole, cannot justly be secluded from it. But (though every one ought to have a voice) *that every one should have an equal voice is a totally different proposition.* When two persons having a joint interest in any business

---

* Considerations on Representative Government, by John Stuart Mill, Harper's edition, pages 179, etc

differ in opinion, does justice require that both opinions should be held of exactly equal value? If, with equal virtue, one is superior to the other in knowledge and intelligence, or if with equal intelligence one excels the other in virtue, the opinion, the judgment of the higher moral or intellectual being, is worth more than that of the inferior; and if the institutions of the country virtually assert that they are of the same value, they assert the thing which is not. One of the two, as the wiser or better man, has a claim to a superior weight; the difficulty is in ascertaining which of the two it is, a thing impossible as between individuals; but, taking men in bodies and in numbers, it can be done with a sufficient approach to accuracy. There would be no pretense for applying this doctrine to any case which can with reason be considered as one of individual and private right. In an affair which concerns only one of two persons, that one is entitled to follow his own opinion, however much wiser the other may be than himself. But we are speaking of things which equally concern them both, where, if the more ignorant does not yield his share of the matter to the guidance of the wiser man, the wiser man must resign his to that of the more ignorant. Which of these modes of getting over the difficulty is most for the interest of both, and most conformable to the general fitness of things? If it be deemed unjust that either should have to give way, which injustice is greater,—that the better judgment should give way to the worse, or the worse to the better?"

Mr. Buckle, in his review of Mr. Mill's Essay

upon Liberty, says that it is dangerous to differ from that great publicist, because he almost always has logical warrant for his statements. We shall exercise all caution in dealing with the foregoing. Mr. Mill admits, or impliedly admits, that in all countries which are about to introduce universal suffrage, unless numbers are counterbalanced in some way by weight of intellect, the latter will effect but little in public affairs, and he therefore proposes a scheme which is utterly impracticable in a country in which the suffrage is already all but universal. If such a scheme were adopted here, it would simply tend to strengthen the party in power, to the hopeless exclusion of their antagonists. If Republicans were in power, they would say that the mere fact of a man being a Republican is such *prima facie* evidence of superior intellectual qualification for political action that each member of the party shall have two votes. The same would be said by the opposite party. Then, who is to judge of this superior intellectual capacity? Party leaders? Then the whole scheme would be but a new device to increase corruption. What shall be the qualification? Not property, says Mr. Mill. Capitalists have already enough advantages under our system of universal suffrage, because after the legislator is elected they buy him up. A university education? How many dunces per annum are turned out by our universities! And as yet, in all our seats of learning, the sciences of political economy and sociology play so subordinate a part in their courses of study, that an education in an average college does not even raise a presumption in favor of the fitness of its recipient for public duties. John Austin,* in some respects the intellectual teacher of Mr. Mill, says on this head: "The principal cause of tyrannous or bad government is ignorance, on the part of the multitude, of sound political science, in the largest sense of the expression; that is to say, *political economy*, with the two great branches of *ethics* as well as *politics*, in the strict acceptation of the term. And if such be the principal cause of tyrannous or bad government, the principal preventive of the evil must lie in the diffusion of such knowledge throughout the mass of the community. Compared with this, the best political constitution that the wit of man could devise were surely a poor security for good or beneficent rule."

Now, it certainly seems odd that Mill—a thinker who is habitually so correct in his reasoning, one who has given his unqualified adhesion to the personal or totality system of representation, and who has proposed a scheme of his own by plurality of votes, to counteract or cure the evils of "too low a standard of political intelligence and of class legislation"—should be so earnestly in favor (before either of these breakwaters to the rule of the Demos is secured) of the extension of the suffrage to women.

To one woman of superior intellect and of that social position which will enable her to form intelligent opinions upon politics who will go to the polls,

---

* Lectures on Jurisprudence, or the Philosophy of Positive Law, p. 289. London: John Murray, 1869.

there will be twenty who will be driven there by threat or promise of reward. A gentleman may argue to his wits' end upon "public duty," etc., with his wife in vain to persuade her to stand at the polls among a lot of men and women who are strangers to her, to be pulled hither and thither, before she can cast her vote; but he can tell his female servants to vote, and how to vote, without much fear of hearing a protest. The laborer or loafer will find, on the other hand, but little difficulty in bringing every woman who stands in any relation to him whatever, to the polls, and thus, instead of counterbalancing the ignorant by the giving of a plurality of votes to intellect, as Mr. Mill proposes, the practical result of the success of the movement in favor of female suffrage will be to give many additional votes to the lowest classes now admitted to the franchise. To test whether this be a true statement, let each man having a numerous surrounding of women, both socially and in subordinate positions, ask himself which of them would most likely avail themselves of the suffrage, if they were permitted to do so, at the next day. The female suffrage movement, therefore, will tend still lower to sink the standard of political intelligence by admitting to political action, and thus to political power, a class of persons who, whether by misdirected education or congenital defect we do not now stop to inquire, would, for generations to come, wield that power ignorantly and under intimidation, and, when not influenced by personal vanity or fear, will be acted upon, with but rare exceptions, in their range of choice of representatives by purely personal sentiments, and not from general or public motives. To one Miss Taylor, Mrs. Fawcett, or Mrs. Stanton, there are half a million of women whose political education is nil; and though the ballot-box has an educational influence, that much-be-praised and overrated education machine is as yet very far from having fully impregnated every suffagan with sound politico-economical ideas; and many a son of the Green Isle has, possibly for twenty odd years, gone to the polls with very vague notions upon the production, distribution, and consumption of wealth. Educate first those who have the suffrage, before you deluge us with a new mass of ignorance. We have already swamped intellect in political life; let us try to lure it back by a proper system of representation before we add so largely to the lower-class vote that we postpone the hearing of the voice of reason for many centuries. We are not opposed to female suffrage, but all reforms are relative in their character, and the law of self-preservation demands that this reform shall be postponed to one which will enable us to some small extent to counteract the general ignorance by allowing those who have studied political questions to aid the ballot-box in diffusing knowledge upon the true principles of sociology.

We would not have traveled so far from the record if there were not many among us who see in the woman-suffrage movement a cure for the ills we suffer from, and we beg leave to remind them of the fact that all political ills are the result of popular ignorance of political science, and that the extending of the suffrage to those from whom it is now withheld is not only the granting of a means of defense against the aggressions of the class invested with political power, but also, from the very nature of so-called free government, the granting of power over those who formerly exclusively possessed it,—a power more or less formidable in strict proportion to the numbers to whom it is extended, and more or less beneficent or injurious in proportion to the logical strength of mind and education of those who are the recipients of this political power. To use the language of Burke, "the science of constructing a commonwealth, or renovating it, or reforming it, is like every other experimental science, not to be taught *a priori*. Nor is it a short experience that can instruct us in that practical science, because the real effects of moral causes are not always immediate, but that which in the first instance is prejudicial may be excellent in its remote operation, and its excellence may arise even from the ill effects it produces in the beginning." If it be true, as the same great statesman says, "that the science of government is a matter which requires experience, and even more experience than any person can gain in his whole life, however sagacious and observing he may be," then what hope for any immediate reform for our manifold ills can we form from granting the ballot to "woman, the lesser man"?

In May, 1867, the Union League Club of Philadelphia offered several prizes for the best essays on the legal organization of the people to select candidates for office. Among the competing essays which were published, that of Mr. Charles Goepp, which we have already quoted, is certainly the most thorough. Mr. Goepp believes the ills of our present system to arise not so much from the majority elections as the fact that the people are not legally organized for the business of nomination, and are thus turned over for the performance of that important, perhaps most important, political action, to the professional politician. To put it in a single proposition, they arise, as he says, from the want of a mechanism by which the people can put men out of office as quickly as they can put them in. Mr. Goepp runs a tilt against those who advocate minority representation, because he believes it incompatible with his system of legal organization. He contends that Mr. Hare's system does not provide for the fidelity of the representatives to the trusts imposed upon them by the electors, and that the voter is disfranchised if the representative does not vote in accordance with his wishes, and claims that for this evil our minority schemes furnish no remedy. "And is not such a remedy precisely that for which we are in search?" We answer that the minority scheme furnishes such a remedy by making each representative responsible to a more compact and distinctive constituency than that of locality, and by preventing the success of compromise candidates, or so-called available men, it raises the standard of political life, and trimming and treachery would thus become rarer than now.

We also answer that the legal organization of people for nominating purposes is a reform which can be introduced *pari passu* with the one we advocate,—not precisely the one urged by Mr. Goepp, which is the return to the Saxon hundred, but such a one as that of Mr. Fisher. Mr. Goepp says that, under our present system of nominating men for office, " good citizens" find no place, and cannot, if they would, take part in that political function; and *apropos* of this he strikes so deft a blow at the cry of party organs that bad nominations are made because the better citizens do not attend the political primaries, that we cannot do better than quote his words:

" This inefficiency of the citizen is not his fault, but his misfortune. It will not be seriously pretended that the mere presence of the good citizens would have had the desired effect. They would simply have swelled the number of wires to be pulled, not at all the difficulty of pulling them; to do more, they must have driven the trade of pulling themselves. This occupation is of a character to be barely tolerable, even under the stimulus of sport or cupidity. Patriotism, as a motive, is not sufficiently irritant in its action. You might as well expect a man, from pure love of country, to beguile his leisure hours by doing the work of a detective, a copyist, or a tax-gatherer. Indeed, there is so positive a repugnance between an interest in the merits of public measures and an interest in the scramble of office-hunters that the two are found united in only a very limited number of individuals, exceptionally organized."

Mr. Goepp's system of legal organization, which

we confess to be a very great reform, to every detail of which we can cheerfully subscribe, is one, however, which necessitates so many innovations in our practices, and requires so carefully-prepared and guarded a law, that we fear its adoption to be very far off. The plan of minority representation is not an innovation upon, but an extension of the system in vogue, and can be introduced and carried out by a very simple provision in our electoral laws. *No organic or constitutional changes are required*, and we believe that power will depart from the politician certainly as effectually as under Mr. Goepp's plan with less innovation. We would, however, deem our work incomplete without giving a summary of Mr. Goepp's conclusions in his own words:

1. *Offices must cease to be held for stated terms.*—This is the law not only of every well-managed corporation, but of all rational private business. No sensible man in ordinary life would appoint his foreman for one year and his journeyman for three years, and make each of them independent of the other and of their employer.

2. *All subaltern executive officers must report to, and hold office at the will of, their immediate superiors.*—This results from the same principle.

3. *Candidates for subaltern executive offices must undergo an examination, and superannuated officers must be pensioned.*—The economical argument furnished by this system against frequent and unwarranted changes is itself of manifest value.

4. *Elections must be held at meetings of organized bodies where deliberation may be had and nominations made, and*

where it is practicable to vote repeatedly, if a clear majority is not obtained at the first poll.—In other words, national and local nominating conventions must be abolished, and the work for which they were contrived must be done by the people in lawful assemblies, always ready to repair at a new sitting any mistake into which they may have been cozened or surprised the day before. The voter must cease to be a lay figure, and must act, in voting, as an intelligent and responsible being.

5. *The chief executive officer must report to, and must hold his office at the will of, the popular body of the legislature.*—This is an innovation upon our practice, but not upon that of Great Britain.

6. *The members of the popular body of the legislature must hold their seats at the will of organized constituencies.*—Without such a provision the legislature, empowered to appoint and remove the executive at pleasure, would become an oligarchy. With it their own amenability to recall would prevent the abuse of their power. There would be no discord between a member and his constituency. Any misrepresentation of the latter by the former, whether from good or evil motives, would be open to immediate correction. The majorities in the house would not fluctuate from general election to general election, but would change as gradually as public opinion changes.

7. *Where a constituency is too large to be assembled in a single town meeting, it must act, in seating and unseating legislators, through the instrumentality of a local popular body, similar and corresponding to the popular body of the*

general legislature.—In other words, the congressmen from each State must hold their seats at the will of the State assembly, and the State assemblyman from each county in the State must hold his seat at the will of the county assembly.

8. *The smallest and ultimate constituency must be the hundred.*—That is to say, it must number from a hundred to three hundred voters, numerous enough to find seats in the same hall, and not too numerous to deliberate without confusion; it must be so small and compact as to enable the voters to assemble without traveling away from their homes, and in the evenings of the week, without prejudice to their daily avocations.

9. *The local constituencies should have their executive governments organized in analogy to the executive organization here proposed for the general government.*—That is to say, the governors should be elected and removed at the will of the State assemblies, the sheriffs at the will of the county assemblies, and the *hundred* at the will of the folkmote.

10. *The entire State, the urban as well as the rural districts, should be divided into hundreds, compact in form, and as nearly equal as may be in population.*

11. *All the hundreds should be grouped into counties, likewise compact in form, and as nearly equal as may be in population.*

12. *An urban community, embracing one or more hundreds, but less than a county, should be called a borough, and one embracing one or more counties, a city.*

13. *Where a borough is so large as to include several hundreds, the hundreds should delegate representa-*

tives to a borough, assembly, or council for municipal purposes; but each hundred should act for itself in the election for delegates to the county assembly and in local self-government. The representative of the hundred in the borough council should also be the representative of the same hundred in the county assembly. By this means the hundreds, whether embraced in boroughs or not, are preserved as the fountain-heads of power.

14. *Where a city is so large as to comprise several counties*, the county assemblies of the counties composing it should often be as one body, forming the city council or assembly, for all purposes except that of electing representatives to the State assembly; for which purpose the members of the city assembly coming from the respective counties should constitute separate county colleges.

There is now before the people of the United States a measure, or rather a series of inchoate ideas supposed to be a remedy for the ills hereinbefore depicted, called Civil Service Reform. The reform has the very formidable and able advocacy of " The Nation," and counts among its adherents some of the best men in the country. It is necessary for us to examine the merits of the proposed reform; for if it will tend to cure the ills of the present bad administration of government, there is less necessity for the introduction of minority representation. If we understand the objects these reformers hope to secure, they are, that no man shall be admitted to occupy any subordinate office under the *appointing power* without first having passed an examination as to his fitness, that the examination shall be competitive in its character, and that the political opinions of the competitor shall be left out of view in determining upon his selection for the office by the judges appointed to examine him. That the right to examine the aspirant for office must be confined, according to the principles of our institutions, to those offices only, for which appointments are made, and for which there are no elections by the people, is almost a self-evident proposition. With us, in theory at least, the people are sovereign, and when they choose a man for public office, no other class of men can say nay, otherwise the sovereign —the people—would not be sovereign. So little is that possible that when Mr. Wilkes was declared unfit for the House of Commons and therefore expelled (whether submitted to a technical examination or not is clearly immaterial), when the people returned him to the House, he was under the English constitution held to be entitled to his seat. What possible examination can there be for a seat in Congress or our legislative chambers? Shall it be a thorough knowledge of political economy, ethics, international law and general jurisprudence? If that be the test, you would deny representation to protectionists and class-interests, and, in short, practically annihilate and palsy the public action of nine out of every ten voters. If this is not to be the test, because these things the legislator should know, then the examination is a farce in addition to being an interference with the rights of the people to have their nonsense and stupidity as well as their wisdom in the representative body.

An examination of elective officers is therefore *not to be thought of.* Very little reflection will convince the friends of civil service reform of this fact. Compared with the importance for weal or woe of the power of the officers who are elected with the power of those who are appointed, the former is so preponderating that the latter sinks into utter insignificance, and the reform of that branch of the civil service which can be reached by the success of the views of Messrs. Jencks, Godkin, Curtis, Cox, and others, is of but little moment.

Let us suppose the gentlemen who are in favor of the reform now under criticism to have overcome the difficulty, that the examiners will be politicians who attain in the first instance *their offices without examination*, either by appointment from some "available man" who has become President by party chicane, or they will, *again without examination*, be elected by means of the corrupt party machinery now in use, and, therefore, in either of these cases, the examination before them will be as much of a fiction as the deliberations of our Electoral College have become. Let us further suppose that they succeed in securing a real and genuine reform of the lower grade of public service, they will, in the first instance, create the anomaly of having the mere mechanical part of governmental duty better performed than the intellectual part, and they will be utterly and completely outflanked and routed by the politicians, if these reformers have really placed an impediment in the politicians' way, by their making the offices to which men are appointed now, elective hereafter, and the board of examiners will have nothing to do. That we are not drawing *a priori* conclusions is evidenced by the fact that less and less is left to the appointing power from year to year, and that arises because the politician's interest is really opposed to it, as every appointment is some slight sort of an examination. Men are weighed, and, all other things being equal, the appointee will be a superior man. It is easier for a politician or wire-puller to put a name on a party slate than to secure his appointment.

"Already," says Mr. Goepp, " even the clerks of our courts cease to be creatures of the judges, and are popularly elected for stated terms. In consequence, the judges lose all power of discipline or regulation over their own official business. The official act of a ministerial officer of a court of justice is, and must be, in contemplation of law, the act of the court. But at the present day, if a judge is informed of the grossest misconduct on the part of his clerk, he can only advise the victim to indict the offender." Of course elective offices will be multiplied, and this multiplication will tend still further to confound the honest voter, and still more make necessary the leading hand of the politician to direct him in his choice. Therefore the benefit the gentlemen in favor of "Civil Service Reform" seek to attain is of small importance as compared with the good to be achieved in the direction pointed out herein, and when they shall have reached the goal, their bread will be converted into stones. They are plastering a syphilitic ulcer, instead of adopting constitutional treatment.

It may be rejoined that, granting everything we say in opposition, we do concede that there is a possibility of attaining some reform, however limited, and that it is of importance to strive for and secure it by what is known as "civil service reform." To this we answer, that every man of weight and importance in the community should not fritter away his time in the vain effort of seeking for a good when but a problematical gain in the event of success can be the only possible result, and that genuine disinterested reformers, who are rare in any country,—and nowhere more sorely needed than here,—should join in securing a reform substantial in its character and permanent in its results.

There is another class of reformers, who believe that no good can emanate from Law, *i.e.* rights corresponding to obligations upon others or all the world, coupled with a sanction. The views of those thinkers are best expressed by Herbert Spencer in his work on Social Statics, and his celebrated essay on Overlegislation. In these and kindred writings the secondary effects of laws are generally contrasted with their primary effects, and an overwhelming amount of testimony is gathered to prove that law, as such, is a mistake and an evil; because it is claimed that man thus interferes with the natural or divine laws as illustrated by political economy, with his own short-sighted make-shifts, which he calls laws.

Thinkers thus imbued regard with a certain degree of satisfaction the evils from which we suffer, because they believe that they will lead thought in their direction, and bring into contempt the whole machinery of government. If you say to men indoctrinated with this theory that our judges have become venal and our legislators corrupt, they are tempted to the reply, "We are glad of it, because a decaying social arrangement cannot be removed by resolutions drawn up in assembly, but must fall by its own inherent rottenness." These same men therefore regard with a certain degree of disfavor any improvement in governmental machinery as tending to lengthen the term of a system which they deem unnatural. They forget entirely the true nature of all law in this no-government idea, and assume the tendency to be the end. Men are controlled in their actions,—

Firstly. By what they believe to be their interests. Now, while the sciences of ethics and political economy are as yet imperfectly understood, their supposed interests are by no means their true interests,—and the province of law is to create a certain degree of uniformity in their conduct upon the basis of real instead of supposed interests.

Secondly. Men are controlled in their conduct toward each other by the law,—that is to say, they will so conduct themselves that they do not become subject to the punishment which the law imposes for its infraction. If the barrier of the law were removed, this basis of right conduct would be removed with it.

Thirdly. Men are governed in their conduct by

the code of positive morality which exists and has force in the community of which they form a part. The code of positive morality may be either sacerdotal in its character, a priesthood may promulge it as part or the whole of a revealed religion, or it may be an utilitarian system of ethics based upon the principle of the greatest happiness to the greatest number.

That the domain of law is constantly receding, and that actions theretofore subject to legal restraint are left to the restraint and punishment of the moral sense of the community, is a fact which may possibly be historically well founded; but it is obvious that not until all men shall agree upon the acts which this code imposes as a duty to be performed, or a crime to be punished—an agreement only then possible when a scientific code of ethics is not a dream but an accomplished fact, and is universally known and acted upon—men for generations to come must be governed by law, must be restrained by law, and must frame laws as rules for human conduct, and punish infractions thereof. The proper formation of the machinery by which laws are made is therefore one of the most immediately practical questions of the hour, and must be solved, or the time hoped for by the enthusiasts who believe that man can safely dispense with law, will be put off for cycles by the intervening anarchy and despotism to which our present system inevitably tends.

What the Antinomians extol as "divine law" is the spontaneous and unregulated action and reaction of individual selfishness. What they belittle as "human law" is the product of the combined effort of human consciousness to understand, effect, and harmonize the general and the individual welfare. The first is at least as human as the second, and the second at least as human as the first. Nothing is further from the teachings of experience than the assumption that all individuals are gifted with an equally distinct appreciation of their respective individual interests. No acquirement is more artificial. On the other hand, nothing is more natural and spontaneous than the growth of law in any community. It constructs itself out of the resistance of the community to the wrongs committed by individuals, which wrongs first make society conscious of its rights. Those wrongs are the product of that very same unregulated individual selfishness, as a reality, which, as a phantasm, the Antinomians call divine law. The development of the law in a community is, therefore, the reality of that very same social ratiocination on the harmony of interests which, as a phantasm, the Antinomians would substitute for the law.

CHAPTER VII.

APPLICATION OF THE TRUE PRINCIPLES OF REPRESENTATION TO CORPORATE BODIES.

The confounding of the right to decision with the right to representation has been carried through all our laws relating to corporations, and results equally serious in their character, and equally mischievous to stockholders as to the voters of the body politic, have been the consequences of this mistake.

Herbert Spencer, in his essays on "Representative Government" and "Railway Morals and Railway Legislation," has treated of these evils with such genius and vigor that we cannot do better than quote his very words: "We will not dwell upon the comparative inefficiency of deputed administration in all mercantile affairs. The untrustworthiness of management by proxies might be afresh illustrated by the many recent joint-stock-bank catastrophes: the recklessness and dishonesty of rulers whose interests are not one with those of the concern they control, being in these cases conspicuously displayed; or we could enlarge on the same truth, as exhibited in the doings of railway boards: instancing the frequent malversations proved against directors; the carelessness which has permitted Robson and Redpath frauds; the rashness perseveringly shown in making unprofitable branches and extensions. But facts of this kind are sufficiently familiar. All men are convinced that for manufacturing and commercial ends, management by many partially-interested directors is immensely inferior to management by a single wholly-interested owner."* Then again: "As devised by acts of Parliament, the administrations of our public companies are almost purely democratic. The representative system is carried out in them with scarcely a check. (?) Shareholders elect their directors, directors their chairman; there is an annual retirement of a certain proportion of the board, giving facilities for superseding them; and by this means the whole ruling body may be changed in periods varying from three to five years. Yet, not only are the characteristic vices of our political state reproduced in each of these mercantile corporations,—some even in an intenser degree,—but the very form of government, while remaining nominally democratic, is substantially so remodeled as to become a miniature of our national constitution. The direction ceasing to fulfill its theory as a deliberative body, whose members possess like powers, falls under the control of some one member of superior cunning, will, or wealth, to whom the majority become so subordinate that the decision on every question depends on the course he takes. Proprietors, instead of constantly exercising their franchise, allow it to become, on all ordinary occasions, a dead letter; retiring directors are so habitu-

---

* Essays, by Herbert Spencer, p. 166. D. Appleton & Co., 1865.

ally re-elected without opposition, and have so great a power of insuring their own election when opposed, that the board becomes practically a close body ; and it is only when the misgovernment grows extreme enough to produce a revolutionary agitation among the shareholders, that any change can be effected.

"Thus, a mixture of the monarchic, the aristocratic, and the democratic elements is repeated, with such modifications only as the circumstances involve. The modes of action, too, are substantially the same; save in this, that the copy outruns the original. Threats of resignation, which ministries hold out in extreme cases, are commonly made by railway-boards to stave off a disagreeable inquiry. By no means regarding themselves as servants of the shareholders, directors rebel against dictation from them; and frequently construe any amendment to their proposals into a vote of want of confidence. At half-yearly meetings, disagreeable criticism and objections are met by the chairman with the remark, that if the shareholders cannot trust his colleagues and himself they had better choose others. With most, this assumption of offended dignity tells; and, under the fear that the company's interests may suffer from any disturbance, measures quite at variance with the wishes of the proprietary are allowed to be carried.

"The parallel holds yet further. If it be true of national administrations, that those in office count on the support of all public *employés;* it is not less true of incorporated companies, that the directors are greatly aided by their officials in their struggles with shareholders. If, in times past, there have been ministries who spent public money to secure party ends, there are, in times present, railway-boards who use the funds of the shareholders to defeat the shareholders. Nay, even in detail the similarity is maintained. Like their prototype, joint-stock companies have their expensive election contests, managed by election committees, employing election agents; they have their canvassing, with its sundry illegitimate accompaniments; they have their occasional manufacture of fraudulent votes. And, as a general result, that class-legislation which has been habitually charged against statesmen, is now habitually displayed in the proceedings of these trading associations, constituted though they are on purely representative principles.

"These last assertions will probably surprise not a few. The general public, who have little or no direct interest in railway matters, who never see a railway journal, and who skip the reports of half-yearly meetings that appear in the daily papers, are under the impression that dishonesties akin to those gigantic ones, so notorious during the mania, are no longer committed. They do not forget the doings of stags and stock-jobbers and runaway directors. They remember how men-of-straw held shares amounting to £100,000, and even £200,000; how numerous directorates were filled by the same persons—one having a seat at twenty-three boards; how subscription-contracts were made up with signatures bought at 10s. and 4s. each, and porters and errand-boys made themselves liable for £30,000 and £40,000 apiece. They can narrate how boards kept their books in cipher, made false registries, and refrained from recording their proceedings in minute-books; how, in one company, half-a-million of capital was put down to unreal names; how, in another, directors bought for account more shares than they issued, and so forced up the price; and how, in many others, they repurchased for the company their own shares, paying themselves with the depositors' money.

"But, though more or less aware of the iniquities that have been practiced, the generality think of them solely as the accompaniments of bubble schemes. More recent enterprises they know to have been *bonâ fide* ones, mostly carried out by old-established companies, and, knowing this, they do not suspect that in the getting-up of branch-lines and extensions there are chicaneries near akin to those of Capel Court, and quite as disastrous in their ultimate results. Associating the ideas of wealth and respectability, and habitually using respectability as synonymous with morality, it seems to them incredible that many of the large capitalists and men of station who administer railway affairs, should be guilty of indirectly enriching themselves at the expense of their constituents. True, they occasionally meet with a law-report disclosing some enormous frauds, or read a *Times* leader characterizing directorial acts in terms that are held libelous. But they regard the cases thus brought to light as entirely exceptional, and, under that feeling of loyalty which ever idealizes men in authority, they constantly tend towards the conviction, if not that directors can do no wrong, yet that they are very unlikely to do wrong.

"Of directorial misdoings some samples have already been referred to; and more might be added. Besides those arising from directly personal aims, there are sundry others. One of these is the still-increasing community between railway boards and the House of Commons.

"There are eighty-one directors sitting in Parliament, and though many of these take little or no part in the affairs of their respective railways, many of them are the most active members of the boards to which they belong. We have but to look back a few years and mark the unanimity with which companies adopted the policy of getting themselves represented in the Legislature, to see that the furtherance of their respective interests, especially in cases of competition, was the incentive. How well this policy is understood among the initiated may be judged from the fact that gentlemen are now in some cases elected on boards simply because they are members of Parliament. Of course this implies that railway legislation is effected by a complicated play of private influences, and that these influences generally work towards the facilitation of new enterprises is tolerably obvious. It naturally happens that directors whose companies are not opposed exchange good offices. It naturally happens that they can more or less smooth the way of their annual batch of new bills through committees.

"Moreover, directors sitting in the House of Commons not only facilitate the passing of the schemes in which they are interested, but are solicited to undertake further schemes by those around them. It is a very common-sense conclusion that representatives of small towns and country districts needing railway accommodation, who are daily thrown in contact with the chairman of a company capable of giving this accommodation, will not neglect the opportunity of furthering their ends. It is a very common-sense conclusion that by hospitalities, by favors, by flattery, by the many means used to bias men, they will seek to obtain his assistance; and it is an equally common-sense conclusion that in many cases they will succeed,—that by some complication of persuasions and temptations they will swerve him from his calmer judgment, and so introduce into the company he represents influences at variance with its welfare.

"To complete the sketch, something must be said on the management of board meetings and meetings of shareholders. For the first, their decisions are affected by various manœuvres. Of course, on fit occasions, there is a whipping-up of those favorable to any project which it is desired to carry. Were this all, there would be little to complain of; but something more than this is done. There are boards in which it is the practice to defeat opposition by stratagem. The extension party having summoned their forces for the occasion, and having entered on the minutes of business a notice worded with the requisite vagueness, shape their proceedings according to the character of the meeting. Should their antagonists muster more strongly than was expected, this vaguely-worded notice serves simply to introduce some general statement for further information concerning the project named in it, and the matter is passed over as though nothing more had been meant. On the contrary, should the proportion of the two sides be more favorable, the notice becomes the basis of a definite motion, committing the board to some important procedure. If due precautions have been taken, the motion is passed; and once passed, those who, if present, would have resisted it, have no remedy; for in railway government there is no 'second reading,' much less a third. So determined and so unscrupulous are the efforts sometimes made by the stronger party to overcome and silence their antagonists, that when a contested measure, carried by them at the board, has to go before a general meeting for confirmation, they have even been known to pass a resolution that their dissentient colleagues shall not address the proprietary!

"How, at half-yearly and special meetings, shareholders should be so readily led by boards, even after repeated experience of their untrustworthiness, seems at first sight difficult to understand. The mystery disappears, however, on inquiry. Very frequently, contested measures are carried quite against the sense of the meetings before which they are laid, by means of the large number of proxies previously collected by the directors. These proxies are obtained mostly from proprietors scattered everywhere throughout the kingdom, who are very generally weak enough to sign the first document sent to them. Then, of those present when the question is brought to an issue, not many dare attempt a speech; of those who dare, but few are clear-headed enough to see the full bearings of the measure they are about to vote upon; and such as can see them are often prevented by nervousness from doing justice to the views they hold.

"Moreover, it must be borne in mind that the party displaying antagonism to the board are apt to be regarded by their brother proprietors with more or less reprobation. Unless the misconduct of the governing body has been very glaring and very recent, there ever arises in the mass a prejudice against all playing the part of an opposition. They are condemned as noisy and factious and obstructive; and often only by determined courage avoid being put down. Besides these negative reasons for the general inefficiency of shareholders' resistance, there are sundry positive ones. As writes a Member of Parliament, who has been an extensive holder of stock in many companies from the first days of railway enterprise,—'My large and long acquaintance with railway companies' affairs enables me to say that a large majority of shareholders trust wholly to their directors, having little or no information, nor caring to have any opinion of their own. . . . . Some others, better informed, but timid, are afraid, by opposing the directors, of causing a depreciation of the value of their stock in the market, and are more alarmed at the prospect of

this temporary depreciation than at the permanent loss entailed on the company by the useless and, therefore, unprofitable outlay of additional capital.
. . . . Others, again, believing that the impending permanent evil is inevitable, resolve on the spot to sell out immediately, and, to keep up the prices of their shares, also give their support to the directors.'

"Thus, from lack of organization and efficiency among those who express their opposition, and from the timidity and double-facedness of those who do not, it happens that extremely unwise projects are carried by large majorities. Nor is this all. The tactics of the aggressive party are commonly as skillful as those of their antagonists are bungling. In the first place, the chairman, who is very generally the chief promoter of the contested scheme, has it in his power to favor those who take his own side, and to throw difficulties in the way of opponents; and this he not unfrequently does to a great extent,—refusing to hear, putting down on some plea of breach of order, browbeating, even using threats. It generally turns out, too, that, whether intentionally or not, some of the most important motions are postponed until nearly the close of the meeting, when the greater portion of the shareholders are gone. Large money-votes, extensive powers, unlimited permits to directors to take, in certain matters, 'such steps as in their judgment they may deem most expedient,' these, and the like, are left to be hurried over during the last half-hour, when the tired and impatient remnant will no longer listen to objectors, and when those who have personal ends to serve by outstaying the rest, carry everything their own way. Indeed, in some instances, the arrangements are such as almost to insure the meeting becoming a pro-extension one towards the end.

"The belief which leads the majority of railway shareholders to place implicit faith in their directors is an erroneous one. It is not true that there is an identity of interest between the proprietary and its executive. It is not true that the board forms an efficient guard against the intrigues of lawyers, engineers, contractors, and others who profit by railway-making. On the contrary, it is true that its members are not only liable to be drawn from their line of duty by various indirect motives, but that by the system of guaranteed shares they are placed under a positive temptation to betray their constituents."

In addition to the evils, so well depicted by Spencer, incidental to English railways and moneyed corporations, there are many others to which American railway-government is specially subject. In England, at all events, they are entirely free from one element of corruption which we have here to an extreme degree. The English railways are built with the capital of the English people. Their shareholders have, by reason of proximity in point of space to the property they intrust to the directors, some supervision over the conduct of the latter; and their system of proxies does not lead to that destruction of all the interests of shareholders which takes place with us, for the reason that our leading lines of railway were mainly built by foreign capital; and in the allotment of shares the American agents or branches of foreign banking-houses have assigned to them, on the books of the railway company, in the name of such firms—which stand simply as intermediary between the purchaser (*i.e.* the customer) of the bankers, who originally buy the stock, and the speculators who get up the railway—the number of shares for which they nominally subscribe.

To illustrate, say that the banking-house "Dodger, Flunkey & Co." make a contract to place fifty thousand shares of the capital stock of the Illinois or New York Railroad Company, Dodger, Flunkey & Co. being the American representatives or agents of the intensely respectable banking-house of Gold, Jones & Co., of London, Berlin, Frankfort, Paris, etc., who then sell at the money markets of Europe these shares of stock; but as the stock is originally issued to the American house, all these fifty thousand shares stand in the name of this house, from one-half to three-fourths only of the men who purchase the shares from the bankers have the transfers of shares made to their names. In the case supposed, there will therefore be from ten to twenty thousand shares on the books of the railway company in the name of this banking firm, of which there may be but one hundred their own or left on their hands. On these shares of stock, no longer their own, these bankers have votes; as the bankers have no direct personal interest in the proper government of the railway corporation, they are of course willing to be bribed for selling out the interests of the purchasers whose faith in their bankers by allowing their shares to remain in the names of Dodger, Flunkey & Co. is rewarded by them in this manner: that they sell at prices ranging from twenty-five cents to two dollars per share the proxies, or votes, on shares which they originally held but are now really in the hands of their *cestui que trusts*,—a treachery for which so-called respectable people deserve the whipping-post or pillory. When some unprincipled scoundrels, who have not within seven-eighths of the amount of money necessary to control an election by the purchase of the stock, or not one-hundredth part of moral character for the confidence of the holders of stock which they cannot purchase, desire to get control of the management, they purchase the proxies from bankers of stocks the latter do not own, and thus, for a dollar or two per share, obtain and hold control of millions of property. Not only under these circumstances do the directors not represent all the shareholders, but they are very far from representing a majority of the stockholders of the corporations they plunder. What is the remedy? Spencer says that these evils arise from the misinterpretation of the proprietary contract. We claim that they arise from a misinterpretation of the principles of representation. And so clearly is that the case that some of the frauds which now take place would be impossible, and all others to which the government of corporations is incident would be rendered difficult in the extreme, if by a reform analogous to the one we propose for national politics, we make the boards of direction of railway and all other joint-stock and corporate enterprises truly representative not of a majority only, frequently attained by fraud and chicane, but of the whole body of shareholders.

This reform can be secured either by the adoption, for all election of officers in moneyed, railway, or industrial corporations, of the Geneva plan, hereinbefore explained, or the passage of a law of four lines upon our statute-book, which shall declare that in the election of officers for such corporations, the number of the shares shall be divided by the number of directors, plus one, to be elected, and the quotient shall be the number of votes necessary to entitle a stockholder to a seat in the board of direction.

In addition, it should be declared a criminal offense to sell or vote upon proxies, when neither buyer nor seller own, either personally or in a fiduciary capacity, the shares upon which the vote is taken or offered.

If the representative system which we urge were once inaugurated, Mr. Burt, the representative of the English stockholders of the Erie Railway need not come here to beg, in behalf of the shareholders he represented, the boon of a single director; but he would be entitled to a director, or directors, as a matter of right, in the proportion which the shares he represents hold to the whole capital stock of the road.

As the directors of these corporations are elected by general ticket, and not singly, they necessarily form a ring, and the thousand maladministrations of trusts are hushed up by mutual consent through a system analogous to log rolling in politics.

All this might be stopped by a single honest director. Midnight sessions to determine upon the declaration of a dividend to affect the stock market would become impossible; carrying to the construction account of the railroad, mining operations for the benefit of directors would be things of the past; reducing freights on certain articles, and thus lessen the income of the road, to the advantage of its governors for the time being;—all these things would, under a proper system of the representation of the true interests of shareholders, sound to us like the tales of the rapacity of the first English governors of India.

Then, again, in addition to making the government of railways and moneyed corporations truly representative in its character, the law of trustee and trusts should be rigidly carried out. To place a trustee in power for any stated period is an absurdity. The election of directors of railways and all other corporations should be by the open vote, and the quota of shareholders who voted for any particular set of men, or man, for the position of a director or trustee, should have the power *at any time* to withdraw their votes and give them to another.

Whatever argument may be deemed valid for the secret ballot has no strength whatever in matters appertaining to the selection of trustees for corporations, and every argument against the ballot has double validity in such cases. We want always to know what the shares and who the stockholders are who keep men in power to administer trust funds when they have proved themselves notoriously unfit for the posts. We want to see whether the votes represent real or fictitious shares. And those very bankers themselves, who, by selling their proxies, have enabled bad men to acquire power, would, by the moral sense of the community, be compelled to withdraw such power and stop such practices when the notorious unfitness of the men thus elected is displayed. Thus, by a simple amendment to our general laws on corporations, these two reforms, so thorough and radical as cures for the injury done to our credit, our financial position, and commercial honesty, would be accomplished. Men would not be more honest than they are now, but premiums and prizes of immense fortunes for scoundrelism would no longer be held out as an inducement to its development, and robbing corporations would not pay much better than the honester, because more dangerous, crimes of burglary or highway robbery.

CONCLUSION.

We have led our reader through all the plans of reform of representative government which have been suggested by Hare and others, and have deviated very far from the idea originally had by the author of editing Mr. Hare's book, in place of which, in the pursuit of the author's inquiries, an original work has been produced. We have laid bare so many ills to which our system is heir, and have dwelt so much upon the pathology of our government, that we doubtless awakened in the mind of the reader occasional misgivings whether we are or are not favorable to what, in general terms, may be called liberal institutions, in contradistinction to monarchical or despotic ones. We do not purpose to enter here into the argument, which we deem closed, in favor of a people self-governed. But we are as yet so far from the ideal self-government, that we utterly repudiate Prince Albert's saying, that "representative government is on its trial." We never have had representative government, and because we do not allow ourselves to be cheated by words is no reason that we are lukewarm, or lack intensity of feeling, in favor of truly popular institutions.

So long as one great portion of our citizens were a slaveholding oligarchy we had not free institutions. And so long as we are under the domination of demagogism we are equally not under the sway of liberal institutions. If American freedom should fail of results beneficial to mankind, it is because Americans have not logically carried out the principles of their institutions. If we fail, it is because we have intermingled meretricious elements which have made us a sham, and national bankruptcy, like individual bankruptcy, may be a blessing, as it also results in getting rid of shams. When our people fail to obtain a government comparatively free from corruption, after they shall have secured a true and not a factitious voice in the selection of their law-governors and law makers, then only we shall be compelled to believe that suffering and experience have not, as yet, ripened them for true self-government. But so long as reforms so evident in design and efficacious in their character as those we have laid before our readers can be secured, we shall continue to hope that freedom may become more than a word, and self-government more than a delusion.

APPENDIX.

APPENDIX.

HARE'S ELECTORAL LAW.

SECTIONS I and II. The Registrars at every general election, as soon as they shall have received the reports of the returning officers of the various constituencies in England, Scotland, and Ireland (to be transmitted to them as hereinafter mentioned), showing the number of votes polled in every constituency, shall compute and ascertain the total number of votes polled at such election, and shall divide such total number by 654,* rejecting any fraction of the dividend which may appear after such division, and the number of the said quotient found by such division shall be the quota or number of votes entitling the candidates respectively, for whom such quota shall be given, to be returned at the said general election as members to serve in Parliament.

III. The Registrars, as soon as practicable after the said quota has been found as aforesaid, shall make and jointly sign a declaration setting forth the total number of votes forming the aforesaid dividend, and the quotient of the same, and shall thereby certify that the said quotient is, by virtue of this act, the quota of electors at the general election for the   Parliament of the United Kingdom of Great Britain and Ireland (specifying the Parliament then summoned, and for which such election is made);

---

* The total number of members of Parliament.

and shall also, with all practicable speed, transmit a copy of such certificate to every returning officer, and cause the same to be published in the London, Edinburgh, and Dublin Gazettes, respectively.

IV. Every candidate whose name is contained in the list of candidates hereinafter mentioned, for whom the full quota of votes shall be polled (subject to any qualification or disqualification otherwise imposed by law), shall be returned as a member to serve in Parliament in manner hereinafter mentioned.

V. Any borough and any parish, or district, or division of a parish, or other parochial division, and any ward or other division of a city, town, or borough, and any hundred, wapentake, or other division of a county, and any body, college, or society incorporate, may, in pursuance of a resolution agreed to by a majority of the electors in such community, at a meeting convened and held after due notice, apply to Her Majesty in Council, by petition, signed by the chairman of such meeting, praying that such borough, parish, division, or body may be empowered to return a member to represent the same in Parliament, and that a writ for such purpose may be issued accordingly at future general elections; and such petition shall state who it is proposed shall be the returning officer, and where it is proposed that such election shall take place, and what hall or public building it is proposed to provide for the same, and the situation of the other polling places, if any, which it is proposed to provide, and in what manner it is proposed that the expenses of such election, and of the registration and record of voters, and the other incidental expenses of such separate representation, shall be borne; and upon the hearing of the said petition, of which not less than three months' notice shall be given in the London, Edinburgh, and Dublin Gazettes, respectively; and also upon the hearing of any person or persons who may apply and be admitted to be heard in opposition to the petition, under such regulations as shall be made in that behalf, if it shall appear to Her Majesty in Council to be proper to accede to the prayer of the petition, and to grant to such borough, parish, division, or body a charter of incorporation (if the same be not already incorporated); it shall be lawful for Her Majesty in Council to order that at all future elections a writ shall be issued for the summoning of such borough, parish, division, or body to return a member to serve in Parliament, and to prescribe who shall be the returning-officer, and any other special rules which may appear to be necessary for the due exercise of such powers; and the said borough, parish, division, or body shall thereupon be empowered to make such return accordingly; but no such order shall confer any right of suffrage on any person who would not, by the general laws affecting the suffrage, be entitled to the same; and a copy of the petition, and of any counter-petition, and of the order made thereupon, shall, within three months after the making thereof, respectively, be laid before Parliament if then sitting, or if not, within the same time after the commencement of their ensuing session.

VI. No person shall be returned as a member to serve in Parliament at any general election for whom there shall not be polled the full quota or number of votes, to be ascertained from time to time, as hereinbefore prescribed, or one of the comparative majorities of votes to be determined from time to time, as hereinafter directed.

VII. Upon or at any time after a dissolution of Parliament, until the time appointed for polling at the ensuing election, every person offering himself as representative in Parliament at such election, shall signify the same in writing to one of the said Registrars, viz.:—if he be a candidate for the representation of any constituency or constituencies in England, to the Registrar in London; and if he be a candidate for the representation of any constituency or constituencies in Scotland, to the Registrar in Edinburgh; and if he be a candidate for the representation of any constituency or constituencies in Ireland, to the Registrar in Dublin; and every candidate shall, in such writing or declaration, state for what constituency or constituencies he offers himself as a candidate; and shall also state whether he holds any, and, if any, what office, either under the crown or in the public service; and he shall also, on the delivery of such declaration, pay to the Registrar the sum of (£50); and the said candidate shall not, by declaring himself a candidate as aforesaid, become therefore liable to bear or pay any further expenses, either general or local, incidental to the election.

VIII. The Registrars for England, Scotland, and Ireland, respectively, shall, on every week-day, commencing the first day after a dissolution of Parliament, on which any candidate delivers such declaration, and makes such payment as aforesaid, and continuing until the day appointed for the general election,—prepare a list of the names of all who shall have declared themselves candidates to represent any constituency or constituencies in Parliament, and shall have made the said payment, stating in such list the respective constituencies for which they are respectively candidates; and the Registrar in London shall cause such list as aforesaid of the candidates for English constituencies to be published in the *London Gazette*, or a supplement thereto; and the Registrar in Edinburgh shall cause such list of candidates for Scotch constituencies to be published in the *Edinburgh Gazette*, or a supplement thereto; and the Registrar in Dublin shall cause such list of candidates for Irish constituencies to be published in the *Dublin*

Gazette, or supplement thereto; and the said Registrars respectively shall transmit copies of the said lists daily to the returning officers of the said constituencies respectively, who shall cause copies thereof to be printed and published, for the use of the electors of their respective constituencies, and sold at a price not exceeding one penny for every complete list.

IX. The names of all the said candidates shall be inserted in the said gazetted list in the following order, viz.: as to all persons who have theretofore had seats in Parliament, in the order of the respective length of the period for which they have been members thereof, beginning with the candidate who shall have sat the longest, and ending with the candidate who shall have sat the shortest, period of time in Parliament; and as to new candidates, according to their age, as the same shall be stated in the declaration delivered to the Registrars as aforesaid, beginning with the oldest, and ending with the youngest, of such new candidates; and where any such length of time, or age, shall be the same as to two or more candidates, or shall be doubtful or not stated, then, according to an alphabetical arrangement of the surnames of such candidates as to whom such particulars shall be so equal or doubtful, or not declared, and which alphabetical arrangement of names as to new candidates shall be placed after the other names in the said lists.

X. All expenses of the erection or hire of hustings, booths, or polling places, and the wages of clerks and officers, and the traveling expenses of the clerk in conveying the voting papers, where the same shall be necessary, to the office of the Registrar, so far as respects all existing constituencies, shall be borne by the several constituencies respectively, and shall be paid out of the county, borough, or parochial rates, or other funds, upon which the registration expenses have heretofore been, or shall hereafter lawfully be, charged; and as to all constituencies which shall hereafter be constituted, all such expenses shall be borne and paid in such manner as shall be directed by the order of Her Majesty in Council constituting the same; and the sect. 71 of the stat. 2 Will. IV. c. 45; sect. 40 of the stat. 2 Will. IV. c. 65; and sect. 88 of the stat. 2 Will. IV. c. 88, are repealed.

XI. All enactments, whether general or special, which incapacitate any person from being elected or from sitting in Parliament, or which impose any penalty or penalties for so doing, on the ground that such person holds any office or offices which he held at the time of his election and stated in his declaration to the Registrar, are repealed.

XII. The stat. 41 Geo. III. c. 63, and sect. 9 of the stat. 10 Geo. IV. c. 7, are repealed.

XIII. If any person who, by virtue of his office, may be the returning officer in any election, should be a candidate at such election, it shall be lawful for such returning officer to appoint an assessor to act in his stead; and the said appointment, when confirmed by the Lord-Lieutenant of the county in which such constituency shall be situated, or by the sheriff of the said county or city, or by any three magistrates for the same county, city, or borough, shall be effectual, and the certificate or return of such assessor shall be valid, as if the same were made by each returning officer.

XIV. Every vote shall be given on a document setting forth the name and address of the elector, his number on the register of electors, and the name of the candidate for whom the vote is given; and if the vote be intended, in the events provided for in this act, to be transferred to any other candidate or candidates, then the names of such other candidate or candidates must be added in distinct numerical order.

XV. The same day shall, at every general election, be appointed for the poll, throughout the kingdom, and shall be specified in the writ; but such day shall not be less than   days, nor more than   days after the date of the said writ (which writ shall be framed and expressed in such manner and form as is necessary for carrying this Act into effect); and the respective sheriffs and returning officers shall, on receipt of the writ and the precept, respectively, forthwith make proclamation, and give notice of the day of such poll, and of the respective polling places at which the same will be taken, within the limits of their respective counties, boroughs, or districts, and for their respective constituencies.

XVI. The returning officer for every electoral district is empowered, at a general election, to take and use as a polling place, to be occupied for that purpose during the day of election, but no longer, upon giving seven days' notice of his intention to that effect, any room or rooms of competent space in any schoolhouse or other building supported wholly or in part by any public or parochial funds, or by any perpetual endowment, or which has been built, or is supported wholly or in part by any grant, under the control of the Committee of Council for Education; and he shall pay a reasonable sum for the hire of such room or place, together with the full cost of repairing any injury or damage which may be occasioned to the premises or the furniture thereof by the said use; such hire and damages, in the event of the returning officer and the managers or trustees or the owners of the said premises differing about the same, to be settled by two justices of the peace, one to be chosen by the returning officer, and the other by the said trustees.

XVII. The returning officer of every constituency shall, at the close of the poll, and as soon as is practicable after the voting papers have been collected, ascertain and certify to the Registrar the aggregate number of votes which has been polled by the constituency of which he is such returning officer, and he shall then ascertain and declare the number of votes which has been polled in the same constituency for the several candidates respectively, counting for such purpose only the votes for the candidates whose names are placed at the head of or first on the respective voting papers; and when the returning officer shall have received from the Registrars their declaration of the quota of voters at such general election as aforesaid, if one or more candidate or candidates shall have so polled in such constituency the quota or quotas of votes, then the said returning officer shall (after setting apart the said quota or quotas as hereinafter directed) forthwith return the candidate or candidates for whom the majorities or greater numbers of voters of the said constituency shall have polled (he or they having such quota or quotas as aforesaid) as the member or members to serve in Parliament for such constituency.

XVIII The candidate, whose name is placed first in the voting papers of the constituency for which he is a candidate, shall be the candidate for whom the votes in such voting papers respectively shall be taken; and if the quota of such candidate shall not be made up by such votes, then the votes in the voting papers of the same constituency in which he shall be placed second, and then the third, and so on successively, shall be taken for him in case all the names standing higher in any such voting paper shall have been cancelled as hereinafter directed.

XIX. All the votes on voting papers in which any candidate is named alone shall be appropriated to him; and if such votes be less in number than the quota, then the votes on voting papers in which he is named first, or first after any canceled name or names shall be so appropriated, and if such votes shall exceed in number the quota required, the number of the said quota and no more (except as otherwise hereinafter provided) shall be appropriated to such candidate, and such quota shall be made up by taking —*first*, the voting papers that contain the uncanceled name of no other candidate; and, *next*, the voting papers that contain the uncanceled names of one, two, or other number of candidates, successively, taking always the voting papers respectively containing a smaller, before those containing a larger number of such uncanceled names; and when it shall appear that two or more of such voting papers contain an equal number of uncanceled names of candidates, *then* the quota shall be made up of the votes polled for the said candidate, beginning at the last so polled which are otherwise equal as aforesaid, and so on to the earlier of such votes in the order of their reception as indorsed on the said voting papers; and for the purpose of recording the said order, and of ascertaining which shall be taken to form the quota in case there shall be more than one polling place, the polling places shall be distinguished by consecutive letters or marks; and the votes appearing by such indorsement to have been last received at every polling place consecutively, according to the said distinguishing numbers or marks, shall be first taken *pari passu; but so much of the foregoing rule of appropriation as directs that the voting papers containing the smaller shall be taken before those containing the larger number of names, shall be subject always to the provisions regarding locality and association contained in Clause XXIV. of this act;* and as soon as the quota of votes to be attributed to any candidate shall be thus ascertained, the voting papers making up the said quota shall be set apart by the returning officer (or by the Registrar, as the case may be); and thereupon the name of the said candidate shall be canceled on all the remaining voting papers, by being stamped across the same by a stamp of a form to be settled and provided by the Registrars, and furnished by them to the returning officer for such use.

XX. The returning officers, after setting apart the number of voting papers which make up the quota, or respective quotas, of the candidate or candidates (if any) so returned as aforesaid, shall, as soon as possible after the close of the poll, transmit the remainder of the said voting papers; and if no candidate has obtained the said quota and been returned as aforesaid, then they shall transmit the whole of the said voting papers to the Registrars respectively, by the hands of one of the sworn poll-clerks, or some other competent messenger, accompanied by a certificate of the names of the candidates for whom such votes are given, and the number of votes given to every candidate respectively, counting only the candidates first named, or first named after the canceled name or names in the said voting papers, together with the total number of voting papers so transmitted, and the number of registered electors who have not polled at such election.

XXI. Where one person is a candidate for the representation of more than one constituency, all the voting papers on which he is placed No. 1, which are polled in the constituencies other than the first for which he is described in the gazetted list as a candidate, shall be forwarded by the returning officers to the Registrars as aforesaid, notwithstanding they may exceed in number the quota.

XXII. Upon the receipt by the returning officer of the certificate of the Registrar, that the quota of votes of any candidate for whom a vote or votes has or have been given in the constituency of which he is such returning officer, has been completed, or that such candidate has obtained a comparative majority, as hereinafter mentioned, and if the member, or full number of members which the same constituency is entitled to elect, shall not have been returned, then the said returning officer shall, if such candidate has polled a majority or greater number of votes of such constituency than any other candidate, *and any of such votes shall have been appropriated to him according to the rules hereafter prescribed*, return such candidate so certified to him, or so many of such candidates as shall complete the number of members which the said constituency is entitled to elect, as duly elected to serve in Parliament; and if the candidate or candidates having a majority or greater number of votes in such constituency shall not have obtained the quota or comparative majority, as aforesaid, then the said returning officer shall so return such or so many of the said candidates, not exceeding the number the said constituency is entitled to elect, as shall be certified by the Registrar to have obtained the quota or comparative majority, and who shall have polled in the said constituency such highest or higher number of votes, exclusive of the candidate or candidates who have so failed in obtaining the said quota or comparative majority; and in the ultimate computation of such majority or greater number of votes polled for any candidate in a particular constituency (who has obtained the quota or comparative majority as aforesaid), the returning officer thereof shall not regard the cancellation of the names of any such candidate on the voting papers thereof, owing to such votes being in excess of the quota of such candidate, but shall, in computing such majority or greater number of votes of the particular constituency, count such votes, whether the same be or be not canceled as aforesaid, both for the candidate or candidates whose name or names has or have been so canceled, and for the candidate or candidates to whom they have been appropriated; and shall also add thereto all other votes of the same constituency which shall be appropriated to him or them under Clause XXVI. of this act.

XXIII. The Registrars respectively, as soon as it appears by the voting papers appropriated to the respective candidates (according to the rules herein contained), that the quota of votes has been polled for any candidate, shall forthwith transmit a certificate of that fact to the returning officers for the respective constituencies in which votes have been polled for such candidate or candidates, stating therein the number of votes of every constituency respectively which have been appropriated to make up such quota.

XXIV. The Registrars shall, in the appropriation of the votes, proceed according to the following rules:

A. If the candidate be the candidate for the representation of several constituencies, and shall not have been elected as a member for the constituency that appears by the gazetted list to be the first constituency for which he has declared himself a candidate, there shall be taken for him,

1. The votes polled for him in such first-named constituency;

2. Then the votes polled for him in the second- and third-named and other following constituencies, for which he has so offered himself consecutively;

3. Then the votes polled for him in the remainder of the constituencies of the United Kingdom in the order hereafter mentioned.

B. If the quota of any candidate be not made up of votes polled for him in the constituency or constituencies for which he has, as appears by the gazetted list, offered himself as a candidate, then,

(*a*) If he be a candidate for a county, or a division of a

county, or other district, comprising within its geographical limits any borough or other local constituency, there shall be taken for him,

1. The votes polled for him in the constituencies comprised within such geographical limits in the alphabetical order of the names of such borough or local constituencies; and

2. Then the votes polled for him in the boroughs or local constituencies nearest to any part of the external boundary of the said geographical limit successively, in the order of their proximity, so far as they shall be included within an area of [twenty] miles from such boundary;

3. Then the votes polled for him in other local constituencies, in their alphabetical order;

4. Then the votes polled for him in the constituencies of the universities, colleges, and other bodies, not restricted to geographical limits, in their alphabetical order;

(*b*) If he be a candidate for a local constituency, but not for any county or division of a county, or other district, having within its geographical limits any borough or local constituency, there shall be taken for him,

1. The votes polled for him in the county or division of a county, in which the local constituency for which he is a candidate shall be situated, in the order of the proximity of the locality in which such votes are registered;

2. Then the votes polled for him in the remainder of the local constituencies in their alphabetical order;

3. Then the votes polled for him in the constituencies of the universities, colleges, and other bodies not restricted to geographical limits, in their alphabetical order.

(*c*) If he be a candidate for any university, college, or other body, not restricted to geographical limits, there shall be taken for him,

1. The votes polled for him in all other like constituen-

cies not restricted to geographical limits, in their alphabetical order;

2. Then the votes polled for him in the local constituencies, in their alphabetical order.

Provided always, that the votes polled by electors of constituencies of England, Scotland, or Ireland, respectively, shall be first taken for the respective candidates for whom the same are polled, who are candidates for constituencies in the kingdom in which such votes are polled, and then the votes polled in any of the same kingdoms, for candidates for constituencies in the other kingdoms respectively, in the order in which the same are above expressed, and subject to the rules of appropriation herein contained. And in order to carry out regularly and invariably the said rules, the Registrars shall before every general election prepare, revise, and jointly sign, tables showing the relation of every local constituency, in respect of proximity to the other constituencies, within the respective limits aforesaid, and also showing the alphabetical order of each class of the said several constituencies in England, Scotland, and Ireland, respectively, and the votes shall then be taken in the order expressed in such tables.

XXV. When the votes shall have been appropriated to all the candidates who have obtained the quota of votes respectively, according to the foregoing rules, the Registrars shall then cancel the names of all such last-mentioned candidates as stand before all others on the unappropriated voting papers, and shall sort and arrange the whole of the unappropriated voting papers, allotting them to the remaining candidates whose names are after such cancellation at the head of the same voting papers respectively, and shall compute the number of votes which have been given for the respective candidates whose names remain at the head of the respective voting papers as last aforesaid; and thereupon the Registrars shall make and sign a declaration, first, of the names of the candidates who have obtained the quota, and secondly, of the number of votes so given for every remaining candidate, which declaration shall be forthwith published in the London, Edinburgh, and Dublin Gazettes; *and* so many of the said remaining candidates as shall, together with the candidates who have previously obtained the quota of votes as aforesaid, be sufficient to make up the whole number [654] of members to be chosen, each and every of whom shall, respectively, have polled *a greater number of votes than any other* of the said remaining candidates, shall, upon the receipt of the Registrar's certificate, be returned as members to serve in Parliament, by the returning officers of the constituencies of which they have respectively polled a majority or majorities of votes as hereinbefore provided; *and* if, upon such computation by the Registrars, it shall appear that two or more of such candidates having such *comparative majorities* of the unappropriated votes as aforesaid, have polled an equal number of votes, and cannot both or all be returned as members as aforesaid, then preference shall be given to the said candidates in the order of their priority in the gazetted lists of candidates prepared as hereinbefore provided, and if the said candidates shall be on different gazetted lists, then in the order of their priority as if they had been upon the gazetted list for the same part of the United Kingdom; *and* to the end aforesaid the Registrars shall, with all practicable speed, certify to the returning officers of the constituencies in which the said votes have been polled for any of the said remaining candidates, the names of the candidates who have polled such comparative majorities of votes as aforesaid, and the number of votes appropriated to them from each constituency, excluding, where two or more candidates shall have been equal, and cannot both or all be returned, the name or names of the candidates who have not the preference in the order of priority as aforesaid; and if they be still equal, preference shall be given to a candidate for a constituency in Ireland before one for Scotland or England, and to a candidate for a constituency in Scotland before one in England, and to a candidate for a smaller before one for a larger constituency; *and* the Registrars shall also, as soon as possible, certify to the returning officer of the constituencies in which the said votes have been polled the names of all the candidates who have *failed to obtain a quota of votes, or a number sufficient to form one of the said comparative majorities* or being equal to one of such majorities, have been excluded *as not having the priority*, as aforesaid, signifying that in consequence thereof such candidates cannot be returned at that election as members to serve in Parliament.

XXVI. After the number [654] of candidates having the quota, or a comparative majority of votes, shall be complete as aforesaid, every voting paper which shall still remain unappropriated, upon which there shall be the name or names of any of such last-mentioned candidates, whether the same be or be not canceled by the returning officers or the Registrars as aforesaid, shall be appropriated respectively to such of the said last-mentioned candidates, whether his name be or be not so canceled, as shall appear, or if more than one, as shall be highest, on every such voting paper respectively; and the elector by whom every such voting paper respectively shall have been polled, shall, for all purposes, form part of the constituency of the member to whom the same shall be so appropriated.

XXVII. The Registrars shall, on the final appropriation of the voting papers, indorse on every voting paper the name of the candidate to whom it has been appropriated;

and after such indorsement shall have been made, the Registrars shall give all due facilities to candidates, agents, and others, at their own cost, for verifying the results of the poll, and inspecting the voting papers; and such cost shall be settled by the Registrars, and shall not exceed the amount of the due remuneration of the clerks of the Registrars attending on such inspection; and the Registrars shall cause to be printed, in a separate book for every member returned under their certificates as aforesaid, the names of the voters whose voting papers have been appropriated to such member respectively, and copies of every such book shall be sold at a price not exceeding the rate at which papers printed by order of the House of Commons are sold; and after sufficient time shall have been afforded for the purposes aforesaid, as well as for gathering from the voting papers such statistical or other information as shall be thought useful, the Registrars shall cause all the voting papers to be redelivered to the several returning officers respectively from whom the same were received, and with whom they shall remain; and the same shall, with the voting papers set apart and retained by the returning officers as aforesaid, be arranged in distinct volumes or files, every distinct volume or file containing the votes appropriated to one member or candidate only, and the votes within every volume or file shall be arranged alphabetically according to the names of the voters; and on a copy of the list of the registered voters, opposite to every voter's name, shall be noted the number of the volume or file in which his voting paper is placed; and the same shall be at all reasonable times accessible to voters, candidates, and others requiring to inspect them or any of them at their own cost, and which cost shall be settled by the returning officers, and shall not exceed the due remuneration of the clerical labor and attention on such inspection;

and every elector shall be at liberty to refer to and examine his own voting paper without cost.

XXVIII. When it shall appear by a certificate of the Registrars that any candidate has polled such a number of votes as shall amount to the quota, or to a comparative majority, and he shall yet not be returned by any returning officer as a member to serve in Parliament; and such candidate, or any of the electors by whom he has been chosen, shall present a petition to the House of Commons stating such facts, and praying that he may be admitted as the representative of such particular college of electors, it shall be lawful for the House, upon hearing the said certificate of the Registrar, to declare, by resolution, that the said candidate has been duly elected as a member of the said House, and such declaration shall have the same effect as if he had been duly returned as a member under the writ.

XXIX. If any member shall after his election accept any office under the Crown, or on the appointment of any minister of the Crown by virtue of his office, such member shall signify the same to the Registrar or Registrars of the part or parts of the United Kingdom for a constituency of which he has been returned; and the returning officers shall cause circular letters to be addressed to all the electors respectively who form the constituency of the said member, intimating such acceptance of office, and acquainting such electors that the Registrar or Registrars will, at the end of three weeks from the date of the said notice, certify to the Speaker of the House of Commons whether any, and if any, what number of such electors, shall have in writing, in a form thereby set forth, signified their dissent to such member continuing to represent them, and also acquainting them, that unless [one-fourth] of such electors should signify such dissent by letter to the said

Registrar within the time and in manner therein mentioned, the said member will be entitled to sit in Parliament, as theretofore, notwithstanding such acceptance of office, and that if [one-fourth] of the said electors should so dissent, then the seat of the said member will be declared vacant.

XXX. When a seat shall, for any cause, be declared to be vacated, the returning officers, on receiving the direction of the Speaker of the House of Commons to that effect, shall, by a circular letter addressed to the electors forming the constituency of the member who had filled the vacant seat, acquaint them of such vacancy, and shall at the same time transmit to the said electors a list of all the candidates for the same, arranged in the order hereinbefore prescribed for the gazetted lists of candidates at general elections, and shall acquaint the said electors that they are at liberty to transmit to the said Registrar their votes respectively, in a form thereby furnished, for any of the candidates contained in such list, and that the candidate having the greater number of the votes of such constituency will be declared to be elected a member to fill the vacant seat.

XXXI. The respective electors forming the constituency of a member whose seat is vacated as aforesaid, may, after receiving such notice as aforesaid, transmit to the Registrar their respective voting papers, containing the name of one only of the candidates named in the list transmitted to them as last aforesaid, the signature of the voter to such voting paper being attested by the mayor, or some magistrate of the town or county in which the voter resides, and the Registrar (who shall be the returning officer in such cases) shall certify to the Speaker of the House of Commons the number of votes given for every candidate by the voters forming the said constituency, and shall return as duly elected, in the place of the member whose seat is vacated, the candidate who shall have a greater number of such votes than any other of the said candidates.

XXXII. A candidate shall be entitled to be, and shall be returned as a member for any constituency in which a majority of votes has been polled for him, notwithstanding that under section XVIII. or section XIX. all the votes actually appropriated to him shall have been polled in another constituency or other constituencies; and in such case the constituency for which he is by this law declared to be entitled to be returned, and the votes whereof are appropriated to other candidates, shall be entitled to return one other member for every candidate so elected, in addition to the number which is to be returned for it under section XXXIII. next hereinafter contained.

XXXIII. Every constituency which is, or shall hereafter be entitled to return a member or members to serve in Parliament, shall be summoned by writ to return so many members as shall be equal to the quotient of the number of the electors of the same constituency, who shall vote at the election thereby directed to be made, divided by the number of the quota for the time being declared and certified according to sections I. and III., hereinbefore contained, and one member for every fractional part of such dividend; and in cases where the number of such electors shall be less than such quota, one member, and no more,—except in cases falling within section XXXII., hereinbefore contained; and it shall not be necessary to specify in the writ otherwise than as aforesaid, the number of members to be returned by any constituency.

SOME CLAUSES OF THE LAW OF 1855 FOR THE ELECTION OF THE REPRESENTATIVES TO THE RIGSRAAD, FRAMED BY MR. ANDRÆ.

18. At such time as the elections are about to take place, the president of the electoral district shall forward to each of the electoral colleges thereto appertaining, as according to the terms of § 8 of this law, the requisite number of printed voting papers, which papers shall be properly drawn out, according to the prescribed form, by the minister or ministers whose department is therewith concerned. And the said voting papers shall be so arranged as that they can be sealed, and provided with the name and the address of the person sending them for distribution among the electors inscribed on the register. A certain time shall be allowed to each elector, the duration of which time shall be stated on the voting paper, and cannot be less than eight days from the date of sending the voting papers; and before the expiration of this time the elector must return to the president of the electoral district the said voting papers, sealed, and accompanied by his address, after having clearly and precisely inscribed upon the said voting papers the names, as well as the position or status, of those persons to whom he accords his vote, and after having affixed his signature thereunto. No voting paper shall lose its validity, even when the voter shall have inscribed upon it the name of only one candidate. But, as in accordance with the terms of § 23 of this law, such a vote is liable to be nullified, the elector who desires to give to his vote its full importance is recommended not to confine it to the candidate whom he prefers to all others, but, on the con-

trary, to mention likewise the names of any persons whose election he desires in a secondary degree, and to inscribe the said names upon the voting paper in the order of his preference, under the name of the candidate chiefly preferred.

19. In case it should happen that an elector has fixed his domicile within a jurisdiction other than in connection with which he figures on the register, it shall be competent for him to obtain a voting paper upon application to the president of the electoral administration of the district in which he is domiciled, provided that the application be made, at the least, fifteen days before the time fixed for the elections to take place, and it will be at his own charge to transmit the said voting paper, properly filled up, to the electoral administration of the district in connection with which he figures on the register.

20. Six days after the date fixed for the return of the voting papers, the "administration" appointed for that purpose shall carefully compare the said papers with the registered list of electors, and the said papers, so far as they shall be found conformable to the said register, shall be transmitted, together with the said register, to the president of the electoral administration of the district (or circle).

21. The elections shall be publicly conducted. The day and hour at which they are to take place shall be announced, at least fifteen days previous to the opening of the said elections, in the *Berlingske Politiske og Avertisements-Tidende*, or in such other journal as may be fixed upon for that purpose by the electoral administration.

22. The elections are opened by the president, who shall begin by counting the number of voting papers sent in. This number, when ascertained, shall be divided by the number of members to be elected to the Rigsraad by the

electoral district, and the quotient obtained, after rejection of any fraction of the dividend which may appear after division, shall then form the electoral basis, in conformity with the terms prescribed in the paragraph following.

23. After having replaced the said voting papers in the urn, and after having then mixed them together, the President shall draw them out one by one, and affix to each voting paper in succession a running number. The said President shall then declare aloud the name which he finds inscribed first in order upon each voting paper, and the name thus proclaimed by the President shall at the same time be duly recorded by two members of the Electoral Directory. The President shall take care to put aside those papers on which the same name most frequently appears. So soon as the name of any candidate shall have recurred a sufficient number of times to obtain the full quota of votes, mentioned in the preceding paragraph of this law, the reading of the voting papers shall be suspended. A further verification of the votes thus recorded shall then take place, and if the result be satisfactory, the candidate in question shall be duly elected. The voting papers which have been verified shall again be put aside, and the president shall proceed to read out those that remain. Whenever the name of the candidate already elected shall appear again upon the voting papers, the name of the said candidate shall be canceled, and replaced by the name immediately underneath it, in the order of the votes upon the voting paper whereon it is found. This second name is thenceforth to be considered as standing in place of the first name, which, having been already canceled, disappears altogether from the voting list. So soon as the name of any other candidate shall have recurred in connection with the number of votes required for the full quota, the same process shall be repeated; and after the result shall have

been verified, the examination of the remaining voting papers shall proceed in the manner already provided, care being always taken to efface, whenever they reappear, the names of those candidates who shall already have attained the full quota of votes. In this way the President and Directors shall proceed until the reading of all the voting papers shall have been completed.

24. If, in the course of the proceedings to be conducted in conformity with the terms of the preceding paragraph of this law, it shall be found that the necessary (number?) of votes to complete the representation of the district cannot be made up, examination shall then be made of the names of those who have obtained the greatest number of votes, and of these candidates, the candidate who represents the majority of voters shall be chosen. No candidate, however, shall be selected who has not obtained a number of votes sufficient to constitute more than the half of the full quotient; and if this number of votes shall be equally recorded in favor of two or more candidates, the choice between the aforesaid two or more candidates, thus representing the same number of votes, shall be determined by lot.

25. In the event of it being found still impossible to terminate the elections by the means provided in the preceding paragraph, the reading of all the voting papers is resumed; and care shall be taken to withdraw from among the names of those candidates, *first inscribed* at the head of such voting paper, who had not yet been elected, a number sufficient to complete the elections. In this case, the decision will depend upon a simple majority of votes. If the number of votes be equal, the decision shall be determined by lot.

26. When a single member only is to be elected, the method of election provided by sections 22-25 is not to be

adopted, inasmuch as in this case the choice shall be decided by *a simple majority of votes*, always, however, with the restriction afore-mentioned, viz.: that in the event of an equality of votes, the decision shall be by lot.

27. At the close of each election, the said voting papers shall be collected, sealed up, and kept for reference in the public archives.

28. The President of each Electoral Administration shall, without delay, make known to every elected person or persons that person or persons has or have been duly elected; and, furthermore, the said President shall call upon the said elected person or persons to declare whether he or they accepts the choice of the electors as recorded in favor of such person, or persons; and if, within a period of eight days after this announcement by the President, as aforesaid, no excuse shall have been received by the said President from the said person or persons, then such person or persons shall be considered as having accepted the choice of the electors that he or they shall represent the said electors in the Supreme Council.

THE END.